D1577763

MAGIC
MYSTICISM

and

MODERN MEDICINE

MAGIC
MYSTICISM
and
MODERN MEDICINE

Irving Oyle

CELESTIAL ARTS
Millbrae, California

DEDICATION:

For Pearl
After 25 years

Interior Art by David Grillone

First Printing, September 1976
Made in the United States of America

1 2 3 4 5 6 7 80 79 78 77 76

CONTENTS

R$_X$

Poor Semmelweiss,
Persecuted for imagining germs
And claiming they were real,
Got himself locked up.
And I, believing he was right,
Though never having seen him or a germ,
Got sick.

Now I'm told by Dr. Oyle
To imagine myself well.
Have I made him up,
A fantasized physician, materialized
By my act of will, wavacles
Aligned to suit my current mood?

A curious cure—hallucinating health.
"I think, therefore I thrive"
(Depending on the thoughts)
Reality reveals itself to be a dream,
The dream and dreamer blend to one.
Boundaries that never were
Blur into a healing whole.

Irving Oyle

This medical mountebank
Has cast his spell on me.
Still clutching my aspirin bottle,
I swallow mystery.
Magic medicine, injected in my heart,
Lights up my tissues 'till they glow
With wonder, and my fever breaks.

Cured of germs and Descartes' ills,
I'll next imagine you,
Dissolve the space between us
Where my dis-ease stalks,
And cure our common cold with love.

—Tom Greening
Editor, the Journal of
Humanistic Psychology

Consider death . . . . As a fetus I am a water dwelling creature attached by a stem to a root system which sucks up life. The water runs out and alien energy surrounds and penetrates my being. My stem is strangled and slashed; the roots of my existence are torn up to wither. Death—birth, a single entity with two faces. A separation. Cleavage which is born with the death of the single celled universes of egg and sperm through their union.

***

FOREWORD

The HEADLANDS HEALING SERVICE was established at Bolinas, California, in the summer of 1971. It was a project of the Church-World Interaction Committee of the Synod of the Golden Gate, United Presbyterian Church. The committee believed the operation of the clinic would be significant in providing a health service to persons who otherwise might not receive it. It was further planned to pioneer new methods in the delivery of health care service to the community, to deal with psychosomatic illness and to maximize the relationship of man's health with his man-made environment.

Headlands was planned primarily as a prototype experimental community health service. Bolinas, California, is a rural area with a population base of about 4,000 people, a typical cross section of which would include welfare, lower and middle class families and individuals.

The clinic began experimenting with new techniques of healing and with methods of bringing the practice to the community. The medical staff carefully evaluated the effects of techniques such as biofeedback, acupuncture, meditation and yoga, as well as reevaluating traditional Western medicines in the light of recent advances in physics and physiology.

The operational theory of Headlands Healing Service was to approach the human organism on the physical, psychological and psychic level believing that, if correctly done, this will effect healing on the physical level. These techniques were developed to apply to the community at large as well as the individual.

The clinic staff was affiliated with a mental health planning team, a group of social workers, public health nurses, county educators and mental health officials who shared the common goal of improving mental health facilities in the area. It was a Clinical Training Facility for students from the Department of Psychology at Sonoma State for research in psychology and parapsychology. Headland's director, Dr. Irving Oyle presented papers in Moscow in 1972 concerning experiments in non-allopathic healing, conducted in conjunction with the International Congress on Psychotronics.

The Headlands medical staff consisted of from four to five physicians licensed to practice medicine in California. They followed the scientific method in evaluating their activities. Criteria for success being based on patient self-evaluation supported by objective improvement in the patient's condition. Case histories document many successes and are readily shared with interested colleagues. An open invitation which extends to healers from all cultures and countries.

Several papers and articles have been published in leading medical journals. Dr. Oyle lectures extensively to various groups concerned with developments in natural healing and related processes, including presentations to college audiences, local citizens groups and religious organizations as well as medical and scientific bodies. Members of the clinic staff continue to be actively involved in international as well as local organizations concerned with the exploration of health care.

ROUNDS WITH DR. JOHN . . . .

In front of the general store.

Young man, long hair, jeans, dark glasses, cycle jacket—"Why the shades, man. Don't you want people to know you're on smack?"

"No. People freak out when they see my eyes."

Far Out!

"Just got over hep. Can you spread it by kissing?"

"All depends on what you kiss."

Out of Sight!

"Some people like to put their fingers in their mouth —you know, nail chewers. Make sure everyone on the bus gets gamma globulin. All the people you love."

Far Out!

Inside the general store

"How's the Mrs.?"

The butcher—white apron, meat cleaver attached to blood stained hand . . . . intense worry stained eyes. "She's got anemia, diabetes, can't sit up, and feels awful . . . ."

Energy Peak

Rage-frustration-terror. Chill shadow of death— fills general store. Too strong: wait outside in the warm yellow sunshine.

Outside in the warm yellow sunshine

HE. . . Yellow beard, long yellow hair, rope belt, beach pants, still looks straight . . . . SHE . . . middle twenties, topless under a sheer blouse tied in a knot across her chest.—Dark, intense, sultry, nubile, radiating sexuality—sweaty palms. "Roberta seems less depressed today. She's out resting in the sun."

"Yeah, I can't help depressions. That's out of my line."

"You did make her laugh."

New yellow Ford Galaxie inches up to edge of beach. Moon and sun passing each other. Seal-watching dog swim lagoon, tacking across strong incoming tide. Mt. Tamalpais, holy to the Indians, glowing pink, yellow and green. Patterned Pacific Ocean stretches 10,000 miles to the horizon where it joins the universe—the edge of eternity. Yellow Galaxie, suit, tie, jacket, combed and set hairdo stop at edge. Motor running, windows shut, blank stares out through clean, curved, tinted shatterproof windshield. 20, 30, 40, 50, 60, 90 seconds. Machine carrying two humans turns and slowly glides back to reality.

On the beach

Young mother with naked baby experiencing sun—scratching—chatting—scratching. A yellow green cloud of poisonous fumes floats up from the city. Dr. John goes off looking for a tennis game.

Purse Snatched, Woman Dies

(San Francisco Chronicle 10/8/70)

MAYA
THE MAGIC THEATER

Bolinas, California

Call it health care delivery experiment. Presbyterians anxious to sponsor. The same people who have fucked it up over the past fifty years are planning imposition from above. Again. Same mindless fund-grabbing "health officials." Multi-million dollar intensive care units. Old men building empires dedicated to keeping other old men secure against death. Cancer, heart-disease and stroke hypnotize hirelings of a dying culture.

Rheumatoid arthritis may be result of immune defense system attacking body tissues.

MIND DESTROYING BODY! *Worry, anxiety, ambition— illusory word monsters in a perpetual thought stream. Body driven by a psychotic, estranged head signals chronic stress, and finally* **TURNS ON ITSELF.** *After all it is designed to destroy the offending organism.*

Susan is a twenty-one year old telephone operator. "I'm tired all the time. I feel depressed." She likes yoga, dancing, and rapping with friends. Walk on the beach, run through waves, chat with old shell-collector lady.

"After eight hours at the switchboard, I'm exhausted and depressed." Sit in front of lean-to on beach— watch seals play tag. Best office consultation room ever. She needs money to pay for a van. Six months from a paid-up, fixed-up, free-wheeling freedom home. Keeps a secret diary.

"Show it to someone else. Otherwise you're just talking to yourself."

"Maybe I'll go to work stoned."

"Make some tea in a thermos, and sip it as you need it."

"Looks like we'll be on strike next week anyhow."

One week in June as the moon waxes: World War II hero killed on business trip; NYC paralyzed by jammed drawbridges over tide of human excrement; Marine pilot does backflip, killing 42 on airliner—no radar; Amtrak does sideflip at 110 mph—no rail; 24 bodies rose up from Yuba City graves, as Mount Etna vomited fire and brimstone. Why, only today we had two earthquakes! Socrates dropped hemlock the way Leary dropped acid, for all to see on NET. War, poison and machines slaughtering millions. V.D. and O.D. "out of control"—Bubonic plague in Denver. Apocolypse, death throes of an era. Something is being born!

New Thought

Last day in June—moon waxing, three Russian Cosmonauts back yesterday from twenty-three weightless days in space. Last time, after eighteen spaced-out days, strange sensations, psychic changes. "Every day over eighteen these men are weightless is a step into the unknown." While he was out there, American spaceman Sheppard didn't want to come down. Consider the possibility that they tripped out and sent their empty bodies back to Earth-Plane. Out of sight.

"The cause of death of the three cosmonauts has still to be determined." "U.S. space experts are certain that the trouble was mechanical and not human failure."

Meanwhile, today, the draft died, Supreme Court saved the republic, and the 26th amendment was added to the Constitution. Dr. John says Mars in Aquarius means high energy in Dissolution and in humanitarianism.

Rosemary's Baby

She was about 26. Six months pregnant without an old man, writhing in the chair with an ice pack over her head. History of good pre-natal care—probably not toxemia. PAIN WAVE One sided, covers forehead, cheek, and jaw—could be trigeminal neuralgia. Right optic nerve looks ok, check left—"Fix your gaze"— PAIN WAVE reaches peak, gradually subsides. I'm looking inside her head. No history of migraine in family, left nasal passage obstructed probably from crying— PAIN WAVE. Dr. John is behind her, rubbing her neck and scalp, loosening muscle spasm.

"Feels better when you do that" pain pain paIN PAIN PAIN PAin pain pa, ...

"Breath deeply." Center of pain localized directly over pineal gland—accompanying light flashes follow pain intensity.

30 second spasms recurring every 10 minutes—Acts like labor. Maybe we can deliver it. Conceive of it as trapped energy.

"What are you giving birth to???"

"The Devil."

"She's Capricorn."

"When I was a child, I read about devils being trapped in people's heads. I really understand how they could have their heads bored open to let them out."

Trephine—If the procedure lasted so long and was so widespread, it must have done something. Devil in the head, an allegory to describe this type of human experience.

"The description is perfect—exactly what it feels like. It's a very evil pain."

Follow the pain, fix attention on it, cannabis relaxes her.

"Starts on the top and runs over my face and head."

Move it, lead it out top of the head.

"When I grab it, to move it, it gets very bad around the edges, and I have to let go."

Move neck and upper back vertebrae. Crack, crack, "Feel the new energy sources and lead the pain out the top of your head behind them."

She closes her eyes, crosses her legs, and sits quietly for 20 minutes. Remarkable clinical improvement.

"It works when I do it, but it keeps slipping away because I'm not used to it—like when I learned to walk."

After sitting for about 30 minutes, she fell asleep. Next time she'll use the baby as an energy source to lead the pain out.

"I'm not afraid of labor, but I'm terrified of this thing."

"That's why it hurts so bad."

"I know."

A fearsome devil, this fear-devil.

Patrick the Epileptic

"Hey doc, can you come down to Scowley's. There's a guy having a fit."

Tie-dyed shirt, paint and urine splattered dungarees, blank confused staring eyes.

"I've had epilepsy for years. Ran outta Dilantin months ago." Note to hospital—Recc; encephalogram, skull X-ray, and neurologic consultation. Probably needs stronger suppressive therapy. Medical Tribune had an article on U.S. Army suppression for 10 years of report indicating that marijuana reduces seizure activity in epileptics. He's about 19, judge's son . . . .

"He's just split!" Far out.

Out of Scowley's, quiet street, warm sun, soothing ocean sounds . . . .

"There's this cat in the garage who says he's been poisoned."

Same Guy

"I was painting and figured maybe I had the convulsion because I inhaled the fumes."

"Get Big Dave to drive you to the hospital. Give them this note and get yourself some Dilantin. They'll check you out." He goes off with Big Dave.

Big Dave is a cycle freak. About 6'6" over 300 pounds, says he is a Hell's Angel. He sure looks it. Carries a huge hunting knife and has a quick temper. Always moving and talking, trying to be helpful. Like chatting with an idling tiger tank. Took a painful foreign body out of his eye last week. Immediate relief after 24 hours of pain and frustration. Felt like Androcles and the lion. "Lemme fix your VW. It's simple, I trained in the factory in Germany." He straightened the front bumper, put the seat back on the runners, repaired the stop lights and pulled the emergency brake handle out by the root in about fifteen minutes. He says he loves little kids and they seem to dig him.

Down from the mesa comes a shiny young Fiat driven by a shiny young man with a shiny young wife. "There's an injured man in the back seat. I found him up on the mesa looking for help."

"You again." A one man health crisis.

"I'm in a hassle with the housing authority. They're trying to kick me out of my house. We have a little girl. A while ago this creepy social worker came with the pigs and just carried her off. Unbelievable! Said she didn't dig my lifestyle. No warrant or papers, just ripped her off. My old man's a Supreme Court judge—I don't know that much, but it certainly looked like kidnapping. I don't dig my old lady really that much. Married her so we could keep the kid. Not so sure I dig the kid. I'd split the scene, but I feel guilty, it doesn't seem right. People always get nervous around me."

The drunken monkey. A crackling energy field surrounds him . . . feel it.

"I can feel the energy building up in my head. It keeps building up and up . . . then I have a fit."

"Do you do speed?"

"FUCK YOU, MAN."

"Ground it. Everybody knows what he has to do with the energy. If you thwart the natural flow, it short circuits in your head and body. It can destroy your physical organism if you screw it up."

The ancient sages called it serpent power. The twin

serpents of the caduceus. Coiled creator of electromagnetic spectrum manifests biologically as nerve impulses.

"I feel best when I'm playing the drums. I hear voices, you know. I've been away for it. Sometimes I have trouble relating at all to the stuff 'out there.' I force it, but then it starts building up in my head."

Once people who foresook "reality" to listen to those voices were called saints and revered as oracles. Whole religions were founded on what we call hallucinatory ravings today.

"Dig it, man, I'm gonna move my drums out. Fuck that other scene."

The Bible says you cannot serve two masters . . . .

The I Ching says "NO BLAME."

"Smoke grass, I think it will help."

Of 103 painful backs treated by surgery 101 were still causing trouble one year later. The search is on for an effective conservative therapy. (Medical World News, May 1971.)

Francine's Backache

She got her head in a very bad place. Social circuitry whirring, drunken monkey chattering and screaming, synaptic gaps cackling incessantly.

"I worry a lot. I can't stop thinking."

All sensory input measured on the procrustean bed of intact   EGO   IMAGE Incrustations of brain barnacles deposited by the ebb and flow of electromagnetic ocean of infinity pouring in through sense gates.

"I can't just lie in bed for three weeks. I'll go crazy."

Slow strangulation of nerve-arteries carrying vital impulse stream to conscious awareness, whose light dims as voltage drops.

"I can't just look at the ocean. It's boring."

Virus-like habit—pleasure—pain patterns reproducing situations which created them . . . sucking attention energy.

"Who's going to clean up the mess while I'm lying around for weeks listening to the wind and watching the damn ocean change color?"

Physical examination revealed a caucasian female in her late thirties in moderate distress. Positive findings included severe restriction of range of motion of lumbar spine in all directions, with a two inch tilt of spine to left. Sensory and reflex changes suggestive of left sciatic nerve irritation. X-ray shows no narrowing of lumbar disc spaces. Herniated disc. Textbook picture.

"I don't trust straight doctors. I went to see this character with persian rugs in his examining room. He hardly looked at me, said I was nervous, sent me home to take tranquilizers: Talk about nervous, you shoulda seen *him.*"

Supporting Players

John is a magician. Appearing and dematerializing silently and unexpectedly, resurrecting dead tiles from their dusty road-grave into a "true game." The sea offers him pieces of nameless ships to adorn his walls, transfixed school of staring woodfish. One energy . . . infinite variety of forms.

Five little old ladies on a Presbyterian "session" council. A house on the corner next to the church. "That house is for the exclusive use of our minister and his family."

Two dogs run across the beach, linear left to right motion against the forward motion of the approaching surf, naked three year old squats on his haunches making mud pies. Primal man examining his environment. He picks them up and slaps them against a wood retaining wall, patting them carefully until they stick.

"You're eight."

and seven people sitting with their backs propped up against the same wall on my right, eight pats of mud propped up against the wall on my left. Fixed horizontal. Advancing and receding vertical of water-boy, adding varying amounts of sand, he molds them till they stick. God creating the world.

"I'm making people, but they keep falling down, so I have to make new ones."

The minister doesn't really believe in God. He's in securities and has this ministry on the side to make ends meet. Lao Tsu the philosopher dreamed he was a butterfly. When he awoke was the butterfly dreaming it was Lao Tsu the philosopher?

All depends on your angle of observation. Point of view, that is.

"I live over the hill, and just use the place on occasional week ends. He has a big hollow inside and would very much like to get involved in something satisfying. He will use his influence with the five little old ladies, but he is new out here. The last minister was kicked out because he brought a hippie-type theatre group in to do a medieval morality play, *La Mama* theatre group from New York."

"You hippies get out of my church. Your presence in the pulpit is a sacrilege!" Like part of the play, far out, five little old ladies. Inertia; negative force. Something to push off against.

Possession—Diana and the Moon Spirit

"Diana tried to kill herself yesterday, and her mother would like you to check her over."

Up onto the mesa. To a large, tree-shaded house with bright sunny rooms.

"She won't leave the house—stays in her room most of the time. She climbed up that tree and jumped out. It's not the first time she's done something like that."

Attractive, plumpish, thirty year old with baggy jeans and a heavy wool sweater with rolled collar pulled up high onto her chin. The tree was about forty-feet high.

"She's been very depressed lately. Has no old man."

"Hi, Diana." Dr. John envelopes her in a bear hug and holds her for a long time. She leads us over the baking sun deck into a small dark room with a bed, chair and small desk. Cold in there, but she says she can hear the ocean. Raskalnikoff's garrett by the sparkling sea. Injuries consisted of multiple bruises of the feet and legs, severe contusions of the arms and shoulders, and a *deep, livid welt around her neck.* She seemed composed, alert, and communicative. Sitting on the bed with her legs folded under.

"Looks like the rope broke."

"I climbed the tree, just relaxed, and let myself drop. On the way down I knew it wasn't going to work. I tried to swim out into the ocean but the sea wouldn't take me either; the tide just carried me ashore."

"Why?"

"I really can't talk about it. It doesn't make sense."

Easy, amicable manner, room seemed really cold, ⅔

"I feel badly about that, but when yo   a strong feeling pulling you from inside, you just have to follow it, no matter how you feel in your head, or how you think."

As she pats her abdomen, I feel a hard knot develop in my solar plexus.

"I just know I have to leave this body and go someplace. This body is a weight holding me back. Fire, that seems right, annihilate and vaporize it, leave no trace. I don't love this body. I hate it."

"If only, I wasn't so afraid of the pain. Fire, that seems right." Her manner was calm, voice composed, eyes clear and lucid.

"Leaving the body to attain a higher state of consciousness can be accomplished in many ways. It is not necessary to destroy the body to get where you want to go."

"I feel I'm going to a beautiful, peaceful place. Home, I just don't seem to be able to get there no matter how hard I try."

"Since you haven't been successful in fifteen attempts maybe you should try a non-destructive route out of your body. All these failures must have a message for you. There are other ways to get to that beautiful place."

She thinks for a long time and nods her head in assent and agreement. The conversation turns to the tarot; she would like to consult the cards.

"I did leave my body once, and travelled to the moon. I came back with a spirit and it's been with me since. It's an evil spirit."

She agrees to go out into the sunshine world, across

27

the deck to the warm light-flooded living room. She seems suddenly free, light-hearted and happy. The knot in my solar plexus is gone. The tarot tells her story.

Covering card . . . . . strength.
Crossing card . . . . . counter influence for good or evil—*The Hanged Man.*
Foundation . . . . . Defeat.
Influence hanging over the matter . . . . . Victory.
Querants attitude . . . . . Power . . . . . She studies and fingers this card for a long time.
"That's really true. Power, that seems exactly right—far out."
Querants House Influence of family and friends, *Queen of Wands.* The watery part of fire. Liability to fits of melancholy.
Querant's Hopes or Fears . . . *The Hermit.* . . Alone on a mountain top holding a lantern for others ascending the heights. Spirit transformed into matter.
Influence entering in the near future . . . Debauchery; seven of cups.
Outcome . . . *Ace of Pentacles* . . . Spirit and matter in a primordial state of unity.

She sits silently and contemplates the cards, touching and absorbing; gathering her own interpretation.
"Beautiful—exactly right . . . Thank you."
The next day, she comes into the clinic. Kevin, an intense young man with serious eyes chats with her and massages her sore, beaten body.

"He has the hands of a healer. He makes my body feel good."

She settles in a corner chair and seems comfortable and at ease. Two young women come in and engage Dr. Mike in a discussion about the clap.

The room suddenly becomes quiet. As he talks, Mike becomes visibly uneasy, shooting nervous glances over into the corner. The atmosphere becomes heavy; conversation, difficult. Diana, legs curled under, rolled sweater collar pulled up over the bridge of her nose. Cold, staring eyes set in swollen, discolored sockets. One of the young women, nineteen, shifts uneasily in her chair.

"What would make a person want to kill themselves?"

The talk winds around the topic of self-destruction like a snake slithering down a tree. Diana sits silently, watching, listening, bruised eyes devoid of human warmth. We discuss ancient taboos against suicide. The young women leave, wondering how we ever got onto that dismal topic, making arrangements for treatment of their disease. Diana breaks her sullen silence.

"I think I'll go out and get some sunshine. I feel that moon energy again."

She goes next door to help Dr. John's wife prepare dinner.

Phone call at 4:00PM.; Margo, John's wife.

"Looks like Diana will be here for a while. She's working on a painting and sort of hanging around, seems quite happy and content."

Phone call at 7:30PM.; Dr. John.

"I think you'd better come down. Diana's done it up in the garden." The knot in my solar plexus. "She hanged herself in the driveway. The boys found her.

29

Each thought the other was playing a joke, gave her external cardiac massage and mouth-to-mouth. Too late. She was still warm though when we cut her down. I inhaled some of her breath . . . felt like her spirit getting into me."
Mother:
"She was like two different personalities, one chasing the other completely different. Been hospitalized, had hallucinations, drugs, electro shock, doctors, nothing helped. It's like she was possessed."

Lilith

. . . . A planet orbiting the earth behind the moon,
The mysterious eighth sphere of the ancients in orbit with, but concealed from the earth.
The consort of Adam before the creation of Eve.
The dark side of the female nature.
The queen of Cups
An archetype with a life of its own
Diana's moon spirit.

Diana; blue, bruised, collar pulled over her neck, smiling faintly. Free ?

An aunt with a soft European accent: "She would be joking around and without warning change, get vulgar and nasty and storm out, turned into someone else completely."
The body is cremated and the ashes are scattered into the sea.

Irving Oyle

*Sitting still, doing
  nothing,
the grass turns green
and spring comes*

*Haiku by ancient
Chinese sage*

*Beautiful mountains
They are amazing and
  great
They come from the
  ground*

*Haiku by Ben
age nine*

Michael has a spider on his porch. He spun his web in front of a window of Michael's house. At sunset the web catches the sun's rays like insects and does a light show.

"At night, I leave the light on in the window. The bugs fly toward the light and get caught in the web; Man, the fattest spider in the county. A friend of mine came to visit for two days. When he was here the spider split. When he left the spider came back."

"He's not in the web."

"I haven't seen him around for a while, I think he's gone."

The empty web still catches sunbeams . . .

Invisible sun
        weaving fuge with red end of spectrum
        on multicolored unseen atmosphere

While

                Dark, dead moon
        freezes incoming waves
                with silver sunbeams
Pink jupiter hangs low over the mountain and
        digs the whole scene.

Irving Oyle

EXORCISM

Rolling Thunder . . . Shoshone medicine man . . . heard about him in N.Y. supposed to have done some magical cures. Met him some months before.
Small, fine boned, about 50, doesn't look Indian. Keeps his hat on and says very little. Guarded around doctors. We share a joint and he takes off his hat. Full, straight, grey hair, strong eyes, sure doesn't look like an Indian.

"My folks sent me away to study in the white man's schools so's I'd have a chance to learn something besides what they teach in Indian school. They kidnap the children and send them to Indian boarding school where they rob them of their pride and history. My folks smuggled me out to some relatives in the city. I took on the white man's ways and forgot about my people. Everybody knows what it is he has to do in this life. If you don't do it you have terrible bad luck. I used to drink a lot . . . I lost my whole family and home. I just got into the car and drove for a long time. Came to this gas station in a town, never been there before. Two Indians, never seen them before, came up to me and said they'd been waiting for me. They took me into the hills and purified all that poison out of me. Taught me Indian medicine. Said I was a healer in other times, and had to do it. I can go out in a field covered with snow and find the herbs I'm looking for where no one else can find anything."

All healing is magic. The Indian healer and the western healer have a common denominator. The trust and confidence of both the patient and the healer. They must both believe in the magic or it doesn't work. Western doctors make secret markings on paper and instruct the patient to give it to the oracle in the drug store, make an offering in return for which they will receive a magic potion. Neither completely understands how the medicine works, but if they both believe, it often does.

"We don't claim to know everything. There is a lot we can learn from you doctors and there is a lot you can learn from us. Our teachings were secret, but about five years ago two stars changed position in the sky. That was a sign for us to come out and share our knowledge."

He agrees to become a consultant in our clinic. Dr. John mentions the fact that he believes he inhaled the spirit of a dead girl.

"You showed me about your medicine; I'll be glad to show you how I do my kind of healing."

An open field surrounded by mountains, night, full moon. Rolling Thunder moving around by the light of a flash light, setting up his instruments. Ten people arrange themselves in a circle. A cabalistic "minyon." Two people to be healed, Zodiacal twelve, the healer makes thirteen.

Richie, "El Tigre," comes from Spanish harlem on a bus with his wife and five kids. Grows vegetables, has chickens, his place looks like a Mexican farm. A graduate of Cooper Union Art School. Active in local politics to the point of precipitating asthma.

"I know I'm doing it just to avoid painting. I put too much of myself into the paintings, and then if someone puts it down, it's like a total rejection of me."

Irwin, about sixty-five, gaunt, nervous, unaware that 1941 was thirty-five years ago. Saw him twice, coming up hill full tilt, face blue, each breath threatening to be his last.

"Helps me keep in shape."

A fire is lit as Rolling Thunder completes his preparations and looks slowly around the circle. At Irwin's face he stops.

"Do you believe in the great spirit?"

"I have an open mind."

The medicine man looks into Irwin's eyes for a long time.

"I can see that you don't disbelieve. That's good enough."

"That's far out, he's collecting tickets." notes Richie.

"Anyone else wants to be healed, say so now, once we get started there's no stopping."

He chants an ancient invocation in a voice which is not his own . . . A puff of smoke from a long thin pipe salutes each of the four corners of creation. Each member of the circle gets a circular marking on his forehead and on each cheek.

"That's to protect you from the spirit when it comes out."

Rolling Thunder asks Dr. John to state his reasons for seeking healing.

"Think over careful what you ask for, 'cause what you ask for is what you're gonna get."

SILENCE

Irwin stokes the fire to pass the time

Full moon, flickering firelight

A sudden brief gust of wind.

"Let it be. Let things remain as they are. Land of beauty, people with love for each other; let it stay as it is."

Dr. John falls silent once more. Dr. Mike asks for removal of fear and paranoia, release of the energy block in his neck and chest so the energy of the universe can flow freely through him into manifestation.

Rolling Thunder spits some water into his palm—stretches it out toward the full moon. Standing silently, eyes closed, turns suddenly, rubs his palms together, and rubs it onto his patient's forehead...again...spit...moon offering...slap of palms...slap and rub John's chest...repeat...back, neck, shoulders.

Crouching suddenly...on all fours, sniffing like an animal...neck, back, face. I focus on flames, moonlight, and forms on other side of the fire—sounds of sniffing—change to sucking—like lips tight against skin—sound like juice being sucked out of a melon. A scream, high pitched, female sound, a scream through tightly closed lips. Dr. John's bass moan, prolonged, mingling with screaming, sucking, closed lip sounds. His form seems to disappear from time to time.

Medicine man stands, eyes closed, staggering slightly and walks silently out of circle of light. More sounds from darkness, wretching, loud, long, violent, back into circle. He raises bird wing and makes slashing motions over and around seated forms. More spitting—sucking—screaming—wretching...three times on each.

Through flames Mike's form seems to have a dark center. Sucking—screaming makes it smaller. Like it's being sucked out. More wretching in darkness. It doesn't sound human any more. Medicine man walks back into fire light exhausted.

"That's about it."

"I didn't know I was that sick," says Dr. John.

"Thank you, I enjoyed it very much," says Irwin.

Mike, curled up in fetal position in his wife's lap, says nothing.

Discussions after clinic hours on the beach center around a philosophy of disease and healing. At this point in human development it seems we are in a position to review ancient and modern healing techniques, selecting and preserving those which are useful and valid. Mesmerized by the early successes with antibiotic wonder drugs, we have put all our faith in prepackaged pills and therapeutic regimens, forgetting the simple fact that ultimately the body heals itself.

"Any medicine we give people is manufactured by their own bodies in more potent form and in exactly correct amounts."

"Disease is a reflection (on the physical level) of disharmony (on the psychic level) of the organism and its environment."

"You mean that head states cause physical disease."

"Attachment—Resistance to the flow of life—refusal to let go—of youth, position, possessions, habits, cause chronic stress and breakdown in a target organ."

"Western medicine focuses on repair after the damage has been done. Techniques like meditation and yoga help keep the organism in tune."

"By increasing blood flow and vital energy to the target organ the powerful reparative processes of the body are concentrated and allowed to work at their maximum efficiency."

Cycles, wheels within wheels, lunar, diurnal, seasonal . . . . We exist at this point in infinite space in an electromagnetic field of unknowable dimensions. To assume that fluctuations in that energy field do not affect human affairs is just plain stupid. It's obvious that the migration of birds is controlled by cosmic events, change in length of day and intensity of light sets off the migratory instinct. In man, recent investigations have disclosed connections from the optic nerve to the pineal gland, (the third eye of lower animals).[Connections from pineal to pituitary give control over the master endocrine gland of the body, cyclic fluctuations in the blood levels in hormones mediate cyclic undulations of consciousness. Our blood is primeval salt water, subject to chemical and hormonal tides. After the fall equinox, we bank our metabolic fires. Bears are an extreme example. In the spring a young man's fancy turns to thoughts of love. Menstruation. Day people versus night people. Wheels within wheels. We ignore these biologic cycles at our own peril. Airline pilots who consistently cross time zones show early aging. Next time you wonder when to schedule a certain event, consult your body—not a clock.]

Phone call in midst of whatever:

"Hello, Irv? This is Nifty Foonman."

" ...." Silence.

"Well, I guess you might not know me... Do you have any bandages?" Sounds like a used car salesman going into his speil.

"My kid broke his arm last week and now he got the cast wet and the damned thing is all loose at the elbow and I don't know if it's a dangerous thing and I don't want to make that trip over the hill and I wanted to know if maybe you had some bandages."

Self-assured rap gradually deteriorates into nervous chatter.

"I don't have any bandages."

"That means going over the hill, huh?" (sotto voice) (full voice now) "I don't know if it's still set right . . . I thought you could just bandage it back into place."

"There is a doctor's office with three competent physicians on twenty-four hour call twenty minutes from here."

"I was just trying to save myself a drive------"

"They make house calls."

"I didn't want to disturb them for nothing."

"You should call the doctor who put on the cast and ask him about it."

"He'll make me come over the hill."

"I think you should call the doctor who put on the cast."

"Do you think Dr. John might have some bandages?"

Irving Oyle

Puma and Stash

"I can't go on living like this. I have to have a decent place to live." Eight and a half months pregnant, huge, matted hair stands straight up, Raggedy Ann dress, soft blue eyes, pretty face under the crust. Stoned old man nods sleepily and goes into rap about revolutionary responsibilities. A Hippie Soap Opera . . . . .

Phone rings, Mary Ministerswife, agitated, angry...
"There's these two people in my kitchen. They just walked in. He bawled me out for interfering with the treatment of an injured finger."
Minister orders them out, albeit a bit guiltily.
"What right do you have to refuse a fellow human being shelter?"
Minister threatens to call police, no more guilt.
Mary Ministerswife: (*still on phone.*) *"They're in the clinic now, and I agreed to share the nursery school part of the manse if there was no invasion of my privacy."*
Now face to face, she goes on to explain that she had a terrible week, came out for a rest and was told on her arrival that her weekend summer cottage had been liberated as a revolutionary act.
Ol' Doc Kind and Understanding: *"Any creature has a right to mark out and defend its own territory. You do, in your own mind have to decide on a satisfactory response to his question. You don't look well, are you sick?"*
Physical examination reveals low grade fever and early respiratory infection. Ol' Doc writes her a prescription and suggests bed rest. He goes through door into

41

clinic to find Puma and Stash huddled in dark cold waiting room playing cards. Outside the warm sun glows.

Puma: *"I cut my finger and found the key over the door. I went inside to wash it in the sink and someone came to the door and told me to tell the minister someone just died. I went back to take care of my cut when they walked in. We have to liberate all these places. It's not even her house."*

After some discussion he agrees that in this instant in time, warming up in the sun had as much to recommend it as did liberating a building. In the course of the next two weeks, they liberate several living places for varying lengths of time until they finally settle down into a nice apartment over the library. Mary Ministerswife does not call back.

Who is this mysterious guru?

Who put the pile of shit in the pulpit?

Will Mary liberate her head?

Is the minister really a probation officer with two other jobs???

What about Stash's visions?

"I was standing by the ocean and I felt all that energy in my body. You know, like rrrrrrrRRRRRRRRR RRRRRRRRRRRRRRR and everything faded away. Then I had this sensation of floating out of my body and I saw God. When I came back, I was lying on the floor and my tongue was all bitten."

She heard voices and saw visions at twelve and was put away at fifteen.

Just like Patrick.

"Remember him, he's the guy that had the epilepsy at Scowley's. The drummer."

The judge's son whose baby they tried to rip off.

"He just got out of the hospital. He had diarrhea for ten days, passing blood, all dehydrated. He came home two days ago, seemed ok, but today he had two four and a half minute fits."

Naked in bed, his words ride on choppy waves of crackling energy.

"I had quite a time in that hospital. That doctor, what a weirdo. I'd been vomiting for ten days with real bad bloody diarrhea, he gets me and shoves a tube up my ass and another down my throat. Shit man, I thought he was gonna kill me. Now the welfare people are hassling me again about going over the hill for job training. Christ, I almost died. Then there's this letter from my father, the fucking Supreme Court judge."

> Certainly sorry to hear about your illness. I must make an important decision about a football match which may involve the state championship. The decision must be made by 3:30 and it is now 3:25. I'm sure you understand.
>
> Father

"He's run out of dilantin."

His wife finds a joint. He smokes it, relaxes and falls asleep.

"Keep him stoned and make sure he gets his dilantin three times a day."

The next day he comes in for a doctor's note to THE MAN explaining the difficulty an epileptic might encounter if he tried to come in weekly for job training sessions.

"There aren't any jobs to be had, the program is just to hassle people."

"How come you stopped meditating?"

"I just went too far out. It frightened me."

"Think of it as a normal state, a power you can control. They say you can travel in time and space."

"I was in this small town in Wisconsin this week. I was actually there. I could smell the hot dogs frying. No one saw me except a dog, a small black dog; he barked and then I was back in my body on the beach. Another time I went back to four years old . . . my old lady says I respond to her thoughts without her verbalizing them . . . One of the things that sets off my fits is trying to hold this stuff back."

* * *

IT IS ENTIRELY POSSIBLE THAT MANY STATES WHICH WE NOW CLASSIFY AS ABNORMAL, PSY-CHOTIC, OR EVEN EPILEPTIC ARE MANIFESTA-TIONS OF A HIGHER STATE OF HUMAN AWARENESS.

* * *

The evolution of this state has been mercilessly re-pressed by forces whose function is to control its rate of emergence, witch burnings, crucifixions, electro shock therapy, incarceration (usually for life) in mental institu-tions (isolation and dehumanization), etc. etc. etc.

In spite of this, the manifestation of this state in in-dividuals is increasing in geometric proportions in our society, bids fair to become the dominant state.

Television has eliminated time and space.
"This is prerecorded. I'm not really here now. I taped this show so I could be in Pasadena. This is next Wednesday, and I'm not really here at all, although I really am here now, or am I in Pasadena?" JOHNNY CARSON. These two factors have been compressed into an eternal here and now . . . discontinuous, constantly changing, always new, always the same; it all exists in your head. There's nothing out there, turn off the TV, click, it's gone. Close your eyes, take a pill, shoot a little powder, poof, it's gone. The more attention you give it, the realer it gets.

India and Pakistan, two of the poorest countries on earth are at war.

"Turn off the TV and come have supper before it gets cold."

James Reston comes back from China with stories of acupuncture induced anesthesia and analgesia. "Mesmerism at its best" says a prominent neurologist. Paul Dudley White! He saw something too! "I don't know what it is, but it certainly isn't medicine," says an English Nobel prize winner . . . .

"There are more things in heaven and earth, Horatio, than are dreamed of in your philosophy" says another prominent English writer.

At a meeting of the local women's liberation group, the ladies are served local herb teas . . . amaneta or marijuanahhhh.

"Can you imagine them coming out after the meeting and clubbing every male in sight?" Some were still hallucinating the next morning.

Magic Mysticism and Modern Medicine

Joseph Akiwenzie

Now, he *really looks* Indian. High cheek bones, oriental eyes, the right color, tall, proud. On crutches with his shattered right leg slightly bent at the knee; the victim of over two hundred years of oppression.

"I don't know much about that Indian culture stuff; I broke my leg in a bike accident last year. I still gotta lotta pain in it."

I think he was a Cherokee; he never really let on how he felt about his heritage. He was there the day Patrick started to have a convulsion after he finished filling out a twelve page welfare application. He gave him a joint and headed it off. I wonder if the public health nurse smelled it when she came in to tell us that Patrick's diarrhea was bacillary dysentary (he sure had incredible grass). Kevin treats him with massage and deference three times a week for about three weeks. He improves, he feels better, he walks better, he sawed one crutch in half and uses it as a cane. He asks Jesse for some more codeine, his leg hurts. Jesse refuses, Joseph leaves. He does not return.

"He was selling it."

India and Pakistan a replay of World War II in a new key, speeded up, in full color. Television War II, it is getting a large share of the total quantum of manifest human consciousness of this planet. If they all will it to stop, place it very high on their list of priorities, so to speak . . . .

"*I'll do anything, doc, just make the damn thing go away!*"

Alan Ginsburg and a bunch of people tried to levitate the Pentagon. Eighteen days after it started, the India-Pakistani war ends.

"What kind of a clinic are you running here any-how?"

"We're letting the clinic do itself."

"My friend, Nifty Foonman called you last week and he says you showed a very hard-nosed attitude . . . . People have their own set ideas about what they expect from a doctor. You can't change that. I remember my old family doctor—you could drop in any time. He'd even offer you tea . . . . Came out anytime, day or night and took a personal interest. Just like a member of the family . . . that's what people expect from a doctor."

"The ol' horse and buggy doctor, he's as hard to find as the ol' horse and buggy itself. We are in the midst of a health care delivery crisis."

Jesse, from Boro Park in Brooklyn. After med school, a year's psychiatric residency, refused service in the war, assigned to our clinic as "alternate service in the national interest." Convinced that his salvation lies in his being "truthful at all times."

"I choose to be a doctor only five days a week be-tween eleven and two. At all other times, my awareness is my own."

"People don't always get sick during clinic hours, you know."

"You mean you want 24-hour—seven-day-a-week coverage."

"You guys are just laying your trip on everyone."

"Middle class people are beginning to find out what the people in the lower classes have been putting up with for years, they never had decent health care. Now they've fucked it up so bad, no one is getting any, not even people in your income bracket." The old fee for service system has collapsed, the doctor-patient relationship has to be redefined.

"Well, if you were running a clinic to encourage people to take care of themselves and teaching them how to do it, I'd say it was pretty good."
To Marcia in Berkeley: *it's a "cosmic clinic"*
. . . "A health care experience."
To the license department: *it's Charitable Clinic License #30001.*
To Blue Cross: *it's "an OEO type charitable out patient clinic."*
To Nifty Foonman: *it's a disgrace . . . .*
To Jane: *"it's disgusting."*
To Jesse's father in Boro Park: *it's a "group practice in California."*

> *It's an illusion . . . It's a dream . . . It's a puppet show . . . Walk out the door . . . Click . . . It's gone.*

THE DIAMOND SUTRA

⸢Thus shall ye think of all this fleeting world
A star at dawn, a bubble in a stream,
A flash of lightning in a summer cloud,
A flickering light, a phantom and a dream.⸣

***

On TV Marcel Marceau dies as Don Juan and comes to life in the next frame as Bip . . . . .
"Don Juan is the ego man and Bip is the universal man."
Tolstoy says literature should serve religion.
Pearlie says "Think of it as theater."
Peter Schumann says "Shit on the audience! Who cares about the audience."

A child is born on Christmas day

Stash goes into labor in the little house behind
Tarantino's, the public health nurse comes with her bag
of tools and officiates. The child comes out . . . the placenta doesn't . . . the nurse considers, worries, starts an
I. V. and freaks.

"We'd better call the doctor, she's hemorrhaging!"

Dr. Mike arrives, disheveled, wide-eyed and takes in
the scene (baby ok, intravenous stand, nurse freaked,
patient hysterical).

He begins running about the room talking rapidly,
offering many differential diagnostic points with con-
flicting courses of therapy, talking to everyone at once.
Someone runs to call Dr. G., a retired obstetrician who
lives in town. The grey-haired, old physician, stately and
dignified in striped shirt and open tie, takes in the scene
. . . (baby screaming, nurse freaking, I. V. running, gesti-
culating and jabbering incomprehensibly—mother even
more hysterical). He picks up a glove, puts it on, shoves
his arm up to the elbow into Stash (who couldn't scream
any louder even if she wanted to). He pulls out the re-
tained placenta, plops it on the table, examines it, nods
his head, takes off the glove, shrugs his shoulders and
walks out without saying a word to anyone. He makes his
way past two fire engines, a sheriff's car, a unit of the
California Highway Patrol, a large group of curious on-
lookers, several dogs, three horses, and a goat.

The next night at 10:30 the phone rings.
"This is Dr. John."
How'd you like to do a suture job."
"I don't have any sutures."

"Puma got into a fight with Patrick and has a fleshy cut on his hand. Stash just had a baby and he doesn't want to leave town."

It seems that Patrick and Puma went out to celebrate the birth. They went to the bar, drank five bottles of wine and got into an argument. What followed then is subject to the point of view of the participant. Puma went home closely pursued by Patrick.

"He said he was gonna kill me and my whole family."

"I was lying in bed with the baby when Puma burst in and slammed the door. Patrick was outside banging on the window and screaming how he was going to kill us all. The window broke and Puma started to bleed from his hand. I started to bleed heavily from getting up and running around. Man, it was scary. Old man Tarantino came down and Patrick split. I tell you, that mother fucker is crazy! He should be put away."

"I was just trying to get inside because it was raining outside. I guess I got nervous. You see, I had no clothes on at the time."

"Man, you should stay away from booze."

It was a boy, weighing nine pounds, healthy, and off to a rip-roaring start.

Later in the week, we hospitalize a big time groupie with hepatitis.

"I'm gonna go back to New York. I hear there is a doctor on 78th Street who can cure hepatitis in one week. I can't screw around with it for months."

Her temperature hits 104°. She goes into the hospital and recovers in one week, still looked a bit yellow, though.

"We were shooting some cocaine. Did you know that some people are shooting into their backs with spinal needles?"

Acupuncture turn-on. Long silver needles introduced directly into the pleasure centers of the brain . . . sound far out?

About a week later, a card arrives from New York. Our hepatitis patient consulted the Dr. on 78th Street and is now completely recovered. He sends us a well-documented scientific paper outlining rapid recovery from hepatitis in a large number of patients on a regime of vitamins, chloromycetin, and steroid therapy.

"He's tried to share the treatment but no one will listen to him."

* * *

Heroin and LSD control pain and anxiety in terminal cancer patients. Eric Kast was into that in the 60's. They made him stop; both drugs are illegal in the U.S. of A. as is acupuncture, grass, and leatril.

"How long are those bastards gonna get away with that kind of shit?"

"These modalities have not been shown to have any proven therapeutic value," they pontificate as they shoot

cancer patients full of "experimental cellular poisons" hoping to find one which will kill the cancer cells before they kill the patient. Think of shooting someone's belly full of radioactive gold. Horrible, ineffective, agonizing, profitable! Radical surgical procedures remove huge chunks of living flesh from moribund patients to no end but the enhancement of the reputation and the bank balance of the surgeon and/or the institution.

 "Pot May Be Useful in Glaucoma Treatment." Lead story, S.F. Examiner Feb. 11, 1972. Other uses include suppression of epileptic fits, that's what they said in the materia medica seventy years ago. Leads one to wonder just whose interests are being protected by the high priests of organized medicine. The crime involved in marijuana use seems to be related to the fact that it is impossible to tax or control the manufacture and distribution of a weed. President's Commission on marijuana and drug abuse leaks its findings in a story in the S.F. Chronicle three days later: "Marijuana is not addictive and cannot be shown to be physically or psychologically harmful even after long use; it does not lead to the use of hard drugs such as heroin; it does not appear to lead to crime."

 On the basis of these findings, the illustrious commission in a "surprisingly liberal report," favors retentions of criminal penalties for, GET THIS:

SALE, EVEN AMONG FRIENDS
GROWING THE PLANT
GIVING IT TO FRIENDS
TRANSPORTING
SMOKING DOPE IN PUBLIC
USING IT FOR MEDICINAL PURPOSES

Even though, Herr Kissinger is treated with acupuncture for an illness of fifteen years duration. Statement released upon the departure of Tricky Dicky for China...
"If he requires medical care while in China, the president will be treated by Chinese physicians in their hospitals."

Stash is placed on a regime of aconite (a flower extract), grass, and thirty minutes on the beach, twice daily, for a condition best described as an impending major freak out. She improves, her hemoglobin rises on iron tablets, her epilepsy is controlled. John Chancellor throws an I Ching re: Nixon's China trip: "It furthers one to cross the great water."

Stanley drops by on his way home after his trip to Russia:
"I told the Russian scientists that we have to remove the mysticism and spiritualism from psychic phenomena and put them on a scientific basis."
Super scientist, dead pan, detached, accumulating data, did a lot of work in Brooklyn on transmission of images telepathically. One person stares at a picture, concentrates and sends the image to a sleeping partner across town. Sleeper is monitored by electroencephalogram. Next morning he picks out the picture from a pack of one hundred, significant degree of success. He followed this up by getting eight thousand people at a rock concert to beam an image toward a sleeping subject.
"It would seem that eight thousand people sending telepathically can generate a stronger signal than one person can."
His next project is to attempt to transmit a picture

telepathically from Big Sur, California to Moscow. Never let it be said that Stanley doesn't think on a grand scale. He also did a great deal of work with Alpha wave feedback training. Alpha is brain wave recorded on the electroencephalogram of people who are in a deep meditative state.

"The alpha of yogis in a trance suggests a state in which all external stimuli are blocked, while the alpha of zen meditators indicates a state in which external stimuli pass through consciousness without binding attention."

"There seems to be some correlation between the alpha state and the ability to perceive extra-sensory stimuli."

If disease states indeed are manifestations of psychic disharmony, chronic tension states, emotional short circuitry (worry, fear, etc., the drunken monkey), cultivation of the state of psychic rest manifested by alpha waves should allow healing to take place on the physical level quickly and efficiently. Electronic tranquilization, no toxic side effects.

Alpha wave training machine. A small computer which receives brain waves and makes a beep when it receives alpha. Concentrate on making the box beep, after a while, you can do it without the box. Will it cure the common cold? Can it shorten the course of poison oak?

At Rockefeller University they have one which beeps when the blood pressure falls to normal. Concentrate on making the box beep. They also have one which beeps when the heart rate reaches a normal level. These automatic (autonomic) functions of the human body are apparently brought under conscious control with training. A fact known in India long before the birth of

Christ,] a concept regarded by the modern medical establishment with the enthusiasm of an inquisitor studying Galileo's heliocentric solar system.

Objective, recordable, reproducable, phenomena controlled by and in the mind. Blood pressure, heart rate, brain waves—Impossible!

How far out into manifestation does this mind control actually extend? Russian scientists report successful telekinesis experiments (moving physical bodies by concentration of psychic energy). Does anyone know just how they do those levitation bits? How about Harry Houdini. Anybody figure out what his gimmick was?

* * *

A twenty-nine year old Jewish girl from Brooklyn gets a new job and a new lover and gets acne-like pimples over her face.

"I just never break out on my face, it must be poison oak or impetigo."

"Sit on the beach for thirty minutes daily and think only about the waves."

Make the pimples go away by an act of will. The same way she made them appear? Ridiculous!

"Remember how it feels, try to reproduce it and get the little black box to beep."

* * *

A car drives by, slows up and stops. Diana's mother. First time she's been in town since the tragedy.

"I stayed at the house, it's been two months."

"How was it?"

"It was ok. I just let her come in anytime she felt she had to." I wonder what she meant by that as she gets into the car and drives off without another word.

ATONEMENT WITH THE FATHER

Patrick gets financial help from his father, the Supreme Court judge.

"When he wants to be friends, the only way he can extend himself is to offer money. . . . He sent a letter."

Dear son:
    I have been remiss in my responsibilities toward you of late. I have fined myself $250.00 and costs for this infraction. The aforesaid sum is enclosed.

* * *

"This old guy fell off the roof up on the mesa, right on his neck."

A seventy-three year old carpenter on his back; pupils fixed, no pulse; heart sounds absent; blue, cold, . No severe bruises or broken bones.

"He was taking pills for his heart, we were working on the job together, been friends for twenty years. He's seventy-three, like me, we're friends, work together a lot."

He was dead before he hit the ground. Cover him just like in the movies; blanket over his face. His co-workers stare in disbelief. The ambulance comes. They load the corpse into the back.

"You shoulda seen them tearing out of town, must have been doing eighty."

"I seen a lotta men killed in World War I, never affected me like this. I know I'm not gonna be able to sleep."

"His daughter was taking his picture. He turned around, raised up his hand and just fell over."

Picture the thing from within the carpenter's consciousness, within his body so to speak.

"Hey Pop, turn around, I want to take your picture."

Camera goes up, funny feeling in the chest, heavy, smile for the picture.

CLICK

It's gone . . . .

* * *

SYNCHRONICITY

A sullen young woman with angry eyes is ushered into the clinic by the ex-lover of the twenty-nine year old Jewish girl with the acne. He got a new old lady and her acne disappeared.

"Look at me, I'm beautiful again."

The sullen young woman sits in the corner and is silent, her escort speaks.

"I'd like you guys to check her over, she keeps passing out."

"I keep passing out."

"Are you taking any drugs?"

"Stelazine, 10 mgm. per day and nardil 300 mgm. a day."

"My psychiatrist at the institute, Izzy Leff, prescribed them for me. I've been going to him for two and a half years now. I went because I was nervous and depressed. I've just been through a messy divorce and my relationship with my parents is all fucked up. We've been working on that every week for two and a half years now. He gave me the pills, an antidepressant and a tranquilizer, and told me to come back in three months for a blood count. He told me not to stop them suddenly as there might be a bad reaction, says people take them for years and years without side effects."

"How much do you pay for all this?"

"$35 a session."

"What changes have you noticed in yourself with all this treatment?"

"I'm still nervous and depressed except now, I faint a lot."

"Looks like your friend, Izzy, is slowly poisoning you."

"He's very drug oriented. I don't want to go back, but I'm afraid to stop the drugs without supervision."

"You should stop taking that shit, and go about cleansing your body and your mind."

From a bearded thirty-five year old cat in the other corner, name of Andre.

"The past is non-existent. You're being fucked up by discharges from your memory banks which keep you from living in this instant. Can you picture what it would feel like to relate to us, in this room, right now, without memory? As if you had just been born, with no past?"

She smiles a warm, glowing smile.

Lot's wife, who turned into a pillar of inert, lifeless salt for looking back. Orpheus, who lost all that was beautiful in his life because he disobeyed the command not to look back. Japanese and German fairy tales with the same theme. Look back over your shoulder, and all is lost.

"That's all Izzy wanted to talk about, the past."

"If it took you two and a half years to learn how futile and destructive that is . . . . Really, to know that; without question, you got your money's worth."

The man in the corner identifies himself as a metaphysical counselor.

"I was in clinical psychology for five years, then I took this job as a prison guard, San Quentin. Imagine what a sink that place is. All those years of accumulated fear and despair. It's engraved into the very stones, fear vibrations, accumulated, reinforced, concentrated. I went up into the tower, gun and all, you know. I started to think about fear, decided I would come to terms with it right then and there, abandoned myself to the fear welling up from the yard and the buildings. I started to tremble and shake, found myself on the floor, convulsing, thrashing around in abject terror. Four hours like that. Then I heard this voice inside say: "NOW WAIT A MINUTE."

The fear left. I got up, picked up my gun and called in for my four hour report. It came back, fear, shaking, convulsions, on the floor again, four solid hours. The voice came back from inside my head:
"ENOUGH OF THIS SHIT"

"I got up and picked up my gun. I had come to terms with fear. While I was on the floor up there in the tower, these words came into my head. Just popped into my head:

I AM
I AM A THOUGHT
IN THE MIND OF A THOUGHT
BEING BORN AS A DREAM

59

> *THAT NEVER WAS*
> *OR EVER WILL BE*
> *YET ALWAYS IS*
> *ETERNALLY NOW.*

Andre gave up his job at the prison soon after.

"I work for this guy over the hill. He owns half the town, wants me to help him relandscape it. Says he'd like me to drive him around. I have to get a phone put in so he can reach me. It's not bad, keeps me in food and rent while I do my research."

He has been going back to the source books of ancient human knowledge, Kabbalah, Hermetic Science, Alchemy and the like.

"I've got the Egyptian system correlated with the Chinese and Indian. When I get my sanscrit Codex and do some few more original works, I'll have correlated twelve systems in all. Aleister Crowley only did three."

These systems of belief—they seem to have some concepts in common:

1) The concept of objective reality, out there, independent of the observer, is an illusion.

2) Time and space do not exist. As we move away from our earth reality, they blend and combine into a single entity, light year. As we move further out into other states of consciousness, they disappear altogether, ecstatic states, dream states, drug states, deeply involved, highly creative states, play . . . trance states.

"I go so into it, that I forgot where I was—lost all track of time."

3) All reality, everything "out there" is the creation of an immortal consciousness outside of time, which it invented, therefore, without any beginning, or location.

4) Each individual as a reflection of the "cosmic

mind," then creates his own particular reality. We make the whole thing up, we can make it do anything we want, if we believe that we can, merely by an act of our will.⁊

"I take a person's name, that's the key to his identity in this lifetime. Each letter corresponds to a number, a musical note, a color, a letter in the Hebrew alphabet, and a major arcana card of the tarot."

From these correspondences, he lays out the tarot cards of the name.

"It gives me the genetic code for any individual. If I correlate it with the time and date of birth, it tells me his psychic makeup, his physical constitution, and his particular relation to the evolution of the species on this planet as well as how he relates to the entire cosmic manifestation."

He does a reading for Marcia. Identifies a "mature, dark woman" Queen of Cups. Marcia knows who it is, some persistent physical problem, and a portent of a messenger, "could mean a child." She hasn't had her period in several months.

"It's a very precise tool, like a scalpel."

Synchronicity. A concept formulated by Carl Gustav Jung. A contemporary of Sigmund Freud. They often got into arguments about dream symbolism. Freud was wont to terminate them by fainting, Click, he's gone.

"Causality is considered to be an axiomatic truth. A great change in our attitude is setting in. The axioms of causality are being shaken to their foundations by modern physics."

"Coincidence of events in time and space means something more than mere chance. How does it happen that they all appear in the same moment and in the same

place? All are exponents of one and the same momentary situation."

At 6:42 p.m. March 28, Jesse talks about the concept of balance in a family, the moon passes from virgo into libra, and the clock on the mantle stops . . . synchronicity . . .

Story on the TV tonight about pain, seems it is epidemic.
"I have been in constant pain for the past seventeen years. I have spent over ten thousand dollars in my search for relief."
"I suffer severe pain in my back for the past six years since my accident. It has cost me six thousand dollars every year."

The case of a man who had phantom pain in an amputated leg is described to a medical school class. They perform a rhizotomy, (cut the nerve where it enters the spine). The pain persists. They perform a cordotomy, (rip out the nerve cells in the spinal cord which supply sensory nerves to the missing leg). The pain persists unchanged. Undaunted, they attack his brain and do a thalamotomy, (fry or otherwise mangle the area deep in the brain which is believed to be the pain center). The patient continues to suffer agonizing pain from the area in thin air where his foot used to be.

Driven to desperate measures, our heroes perform the piece de resistance of psychosurgery, a prefrontal lobotomy. This consists of shoving a sharp instrument into the victim's eye socket and clawing out the nerve tracts which connect the highest centers of consciousness with the rest of the brain.

In the course of this procedure "there is induced a state of docility and tameness. It also produces loss of emotion, spontaneity, and fantasy life. Insight and creativity are destroyed."

"The patient continued to suffer severe and intractible phantom pain."

Hippocrates admonished his students to do nothing rather than to make matters worse. He obviously reckoned without the profit motive.

Scene switch to tall, skinny man in white coat and a frozen, blank face explaining how he put platinum electrodes under the scalp of the extremely obese subject, stripped to the waist, redundant belly and pendulous breasts, a steel claw where his right hand should be.

"From these electrodes, a wire runs over the shoulder, down the chest, all this under the skin, of course, to connect with a sensor which is implanted in the chest wall."

A large bulky control box carried in the pocket, sends a signal to the receiver which transmits an electrical charge to the electrodes and to the base of the brain.

"Tell us, sir, what your trouble was, and how the treatment helped you."

Sounds like a commercial.

"After I lost my arm, I continued to have this terrible pain in the last two fingers of the hand."

"You continued to suffer pain in a non-existent hand."

Now it looks like a comedy team doing a sick joke.

"Yeah."

"What happens now, when you get this phantom pain?"

"I just push this button and the pain gets less. You may think this is crazy, but it feels just like a bunch of ants are crawling up my arm."

A testimonial from a satisfied user . . . . I wonder what it feels like to have an electrode under your scalp, a wire under your skin, and an electrical sensor implanted in your chest.

Francine having graciously refused the offer of an orthopedic surgeon to tear out the roof over her lower spinal cord, sheds her middle class responsibilities, her husband and her back pain, gradually, over a period of six months . . .

"I'm finally free at 42!"

In a reversal of your traditional generation gap script, her fifteen year old daughter looks on with alarm.

"Look at you carrying on, smoking dope and dressing like a middle-aged gypsy."

THE FACT IS, SHE REALLY LOOKS GREAT!

Grandpa finds some seeds

"What are these?"

"Marijuana seeds."

"What are you going to do with them?"

"Plant them and smoke it."

"Are you crazy? Think of the children!"

The American Medical Association is considering inviting Chinese acupuncturists to lecture at their next convention and to demonstrate their techniques for the relief of pain.

"Are you crazy? Think of the anesthesiologists!"

* * *

Probably the main reason people seek medical help is for the relief of pain. This has been true since the beginning of healing. Consider the millions of people spending untold sums of money in an unsuccessful quest for pain relief. Heroin is, after all, a potent pain killer... as is alcohol.

Contemplate the spectacle of a massive, pompous, health care elite which claims to be the best of all possible health care elites; contemptuous of the past, unrelated to the future, and blind to the present.

THEY HAVE NO KNOWLEDGE OF THE NATURE OR TREATMENT OF CHRONIC PAIN.

"All the known pain pathways in this patient were removed, and yet his phantom pain persisted. We must revise our concepts as to the nature and location of the sensation of pain."

Psychics report the persistence of the aura in the area of a missing limb. Russian scientists photograph energy fields around physical objects. In a high intensity electrical field, the human body emits colored energy, resembles the color aura seen by clairvoyants and others.

"It is a high energy field which surrounds and interpenetrates the physical substance of the human body" . . Paracelsus, the father of modern chemotherapeutics, giant figure in the history of western medicine postulated an auric body like that back in the 1500's. This bioplasmic energy seems to have some fascinating characteristics.

It is concentrated along the acupuncture points described by ancient Chinese medicine.

It responds instantly to bursts of solar energy.

It shows change which in several days is reflected in change in the bodily states of health.

It may be the energy responsible for telepathy and ESP.

The Russians no longer question the existence of this form of energy. They bring to bear the full force of their computer technology on the problem of finding practical applications. A meeting is called in Moscow with U.S. parapsychologists. Stanley sends an invitation to join a panel on "Applications of bioplasmic energy in healing . . . . Paranormal Healing In A Free People's Clinic."

It costs $1500 for the trip . . . ask the synod to front it. They're cutting salaries to keep the budget down. Send a deposit anyway. Passport still good, the fare will materialize.

Reflections on Insanity

A discussion on the cost of medical care on TV. Working man's family with $14,000 per year income.

The father says, "I was prepared to pay the cost for delivery of a normal baby, $1000."

"I thought it was free to have your own baby," says Ben.

Ben is only 10. What does he know. Think of the children.

His child had a cogenital defect. Insurance companies exclude the first two weeks of the newborn's life.

"We didn't think of the cost," the mother's voice was anguished. "We just knew he had to be helped." The cost was twelve thousand dollars.

"It just means eating beans instead of meat for awhile . . . if the hospitals will wait. Otherwise, we'll have to sell everything we have."

Consummate skill . . . saving the life of an infant, and relegating him to the life of a pauper. Poor nutrition up to the eighth month of life may result in fewer brain cells and decreased intelligence, fewer circuits.

The social worker advises, "The best course for this family would be to seek assistance from state welfare agencies."

What were their motives in saving that child's life?

* * *

A small stocky lady in a blue dress appears on the beach carrying a pail full of dead sharks.

"I'm surprised they let me come this far alone. Could you please take my picture so I can prove I was here. I'm a nun . . . they didn't allow us out like this before . . . things are certainly changing. The priests used to order us about just because we were women. I don't like that and I tell them so. We used to keep everything inside, but now we just speak right out, like at table I said, "Sister, please stop that, you're bugging me." Even when mother superior says something stupid, I'm not afraid to tell her now. I'm in the church for life . . keep my independence; always did . . . you can't change anything by running away from it . . . nice talking to you."

"Faster, faster," said the red queen.

"I'm running as fast as I can, but we don't seem to be getting anyplace."

"My dear, you have to run as fast as you can just to keep from falling behind!" said the red queen . . . to Alice . . . in wonderland.

* * *

The California prison system is planning behavior modification centers for recalcitrant and hostile prisoners. They mean psychosurgery.

Birth-death . . . future shock . . . change with ever increasing speed. The dying reality fights ruthlessly against its own rebirth . . . a quantum jump in consciousness. Everybody is stoned! Millions of urban dwellers and down-home country folk are experiencing altered states of consciousness. At the dentist, they sniff nitrous oxide. In the cities, as hydrocarbon and carbon monoxide levels are cut by smog devices on cars, the levels of oxides of nitrogen rise in equal proportion, among them nitrous oxide. Stoned on smog! Far out.

Ketamine, safest anesthetic around outside of acu-puncture. Any middle class folk going into a hospital for minor to moderate surgical procedures are likely to get this anesthetic. When the patient comes out, he has a psychedelic experience:

    "Hey doc, you know you're square?"

    "Sorry, I'll practice up on my hip."

    "No, I mean your shape. Your body is square."

See the square shaped doctor . . . feel the pain in the phantom limb . . . . Reality concepts changing with ever increasing speed. The wheel is spinning faster and faster . . . people spinning out of their bodies.

***

Thirty year old mother of two from Alabama, her name is Gerta.

"I was lying in bed and I felt a snap and there I was, up on the ceiling looking at my body lying in the bed. It was scary!"

"I lie on my back, at a time when I'm not sleepy, close my eyes and concentrate on one part of my body at a time, bring it into full attention and then relax it completely. Then I focus my eyes on the center of my forehead and everything becomes purple. When I'm in the purple space I realize that I'm no longer in my body. In that space I can ask for guidance and I always get it."

"You guys better do something for her . . . she's crazier than anyone I ever met, in or out of the institution." Patrick . . . who's been there.

Gerta comes in, dripping wet . . . she's been in the lagoon.

"I'm cold . . . gimme a cigarette . . . don't touch me . . . I'm fine!"

"She left her kids with a friend three days ago and never came back."

"I saw the snake by the side of my bed and I was afraid . . . the wheel is broken . . . this is here and now, this is heaven. Who are you?"

"Do you know the date today?"

She knows the date . . . "Don't be stupid . . . DON'T LOOK AT ME!" Someone embraces her; she goes limp.

"This girl needs to be hospitalized."

"Must we? Hospitals are so dreadful." Helia, looks like she stepped out of a Beardsley drawing, keeps the records, fills out Blue Cross forms, fills capsules with golden seal powder, reads horoscopes, astrologic birth control, and stands silently inside of hollow trees.

Someone plays the piano for a while; someone else reads Blake's "Songs of Innocence." A calm settles over the room.

Jesse leaves to arrange transportation to the hospital. . . .

FIRE DEPARTMENT

"Sure, we respond to emergencies, but our ambulance is not for transporting mental cases." Like he was talking about lepers.

POLICE DEPARTMENT

"We won't transport a mental case unless they've committed a crime."

MENTAL HEALTH DEPARTMENT

"Just bring her right on in and we'll take care of her."

***

A different reality structure is even more terrifying than a different skin color . . . to "normal" or "usual" people . . . .

70

News Item: "There are sixty million people in the United States who must be considered mentally ill" . . . . That is, one member of each American family is considered crazy by someone's psychiatric standards.

"Everyone is crazy, my friend, except me and thee, and I'm beginning to wonder about thee."

In your average run of the mill nut house the best way to tell the patients from the staff is to check to see which ones are carrying keys!

I wonder if they include those cats dropping napalm on their fellow humans . . . nursemaids to a computer.

"I just do my job to the best of my ability."

Ford calls back the entire run of Montegos and Torinos . . . the rear wheels have a tendency to fall off on a curve. The original plan was to install a loud horn which would sound when that was about to happen. "When you test drive a Torino, you're in for a big surprise!"

Three astronauts head for earth, grumpy and tired after taking pictures of each other saluting a plastic flag nobly waving in a non-existent atmosphere.

Someone claims to have discovered a new planet with the aid of a computer.

* * *

"Can you tell me what would make a baby's eyes all red, you know, like she has a hangover? She breathes funny too, makes this weird wheezing sound. I have to hang around all day and answer these stupid phone calls. We had her room painted about a week ago. Gold, not gold paint, real gold, dissolved in this evil smelling stuff. It's real powerful. You can still smell it. Anyway, that's when she got sick about a week ago. I wonder if it could be the paint."

Nifty Foonman drops in to check out our alpha machine. He has six kids, used to be in clothing in New York, freaked out and went on welfare, helping the two kids who bought the general store, teaching them retail techniques.

"Whenever you see the prices drop suddenly, you know it's Nifty's work." *He's been in 'subud' for twelve years. Puts himself in the 'latihan' state and produced 80% beta waves. Beta is a wave of over thirteen cycles indicating a state of focused attention. A psychic lady in a light trance produced the same result, focused attention. Nifty is upset because he can't do 100% of four different brain waves simultaneously.*

"Subud is a bunch of people getting together in a large room. Maybe they push the tables out of the way, open themselves to receive 'latihan.' Something takes over their bodies; maybe your hand will start a certain movement on its own. Sometimes it's screaming. Sometimes it's thrashing around on the floor. You just open to it and it comes to you. One girl just slept. She would fall asleep when it started and sleep for exactly 30 minutes. . . kept that up at every meeting for years. The movements or possession keeps up until the accumulated crap built up since the previous meeting all works itself out."

An art major hooks himself up to six alpha machines at once.

"Oh yes, we're very compatible you see, he's a very high alpha producer."

"We stand on the brink of World War III."

The killer climbs up the cliff and enters the home of a young family. His hands and clothes are covered with blood.

"I was climbing on the cliff and I cut myself."

She helps him get cleaned up and gives him some clothes.

"Thanks, I'm on my way to San Francisco."

"Can you give Bobby a lift? He's going in to meet his father."

The murderer drops the eight-year-old off in town after a pleasant and chatty drive over the mountain.

"They picked him up in Berkeley. Had his description."

George Wallace, macho champion son of a fighter, meets him in Maryland.

"I would consider him to be a dull, normal individual. He's not the brightest guy in the world, but I wouldn't call him abnormal at all."

He was in my gym class in high school. He was very competitive, liked sports, got along well. Very competitive . . . very competitive."

News photos show him at Wallace rallies on several dates. He asks a guard to lead the governor in his direction. He would just like to shake his hand.

"It appears he had been stalking his victim for some time."

Richard Speck, George Whitcomb, short hair, dull, normal, average American kid, very competitive. Maybe it's an extra XX chromosome. Careful, now, it's come off the TV screen into our little town!

We keep taking the road signs down, but somehow he found his way here.

In one single instant, George C. Wallace reaches the pinnacle of his political career and loses the use of his legs. BANG! It's gone.

In L.A. someone mentions to a cop that something funny is happening in the bank. Two more airliners are highjacked. Desperation is in the air . . . .

Our alpha machine is reclaimed by the donator for use in a promotional demonstration in New York. "We only lent it to you, after all, our prime purpose in this thing is to make money."

This whole thing is happening on the 'Titanic'...

Maybe the only ones to survive will be those who can leave their bodies.

The orbit of the new planet, some call it Vulcan, moves in a direction opposite to the others in our solar system. It may have been trapped by our solar system, a visitor from outer space so to speak. The clue was the aberrant arrival of Haley's comet. When it arrived later than calculations indicated that it would. The comet couldn't be wrong; the calculations seem accurate. There must be another factor not considered... ask the oracle. The computer worked on the problem for 100 hours, at a rate one million times faster than the earliest computers of twenty years ago and postulated the existence of a planet three hundred times the size of earth, moving in a retrograde direction. How long has it been there?

Michael moves away from the house he shared with the spider.

"His name was Charlie."

He creates a beautiful garden. A peacock flies into it one day and stays.

"His name is Desmond, I've been trying to find a mate for him, but it's not easy to find a female peacock in California."

"Did you hear about the murder on the beach?"

The cook at the local eatery washes up with the tide.

"He was beaten and stabbed with a club, and thrown into the ocean."

"He was my friend! I saw this creep stalking my friend. He was only in town one week . . . from North Carolina . . . fresh out of the nut house. He followed my friend to the beach . . . stalked him like an animal . . . stalked him and killed him. He killed my friend . . . shit!"

Does a mad killer stalk the streets of our little town?

"He was living with Al and his old lady. She's a blind chick. He's been there about a week. He started to bug the chick and they asked him to leave but he kept breaking into the house. They called the cops. He drove off; but several people saw him come back and follow Al onto the beach. The cops made a composite picture from their descriptions."

* * *

Masked robots in winged giant computers rain thirty tons of bombs apiece on a town called An Loc, a city called Hanoi, and the city called Haiphong. A physician reports that the bombs contain plastic pellets which penetrate human flesh, but do not show up on X-ray.

"Makes the job of removing them incredibly difficult."

* * *

"Can you give me a prescription for valium. I thought I would patronize the local medical establishment."

"I don't write for valium."

"Why not?"

"It has too many toxic side effects, and I don't write for drugs that I wouldn't take myself."

"Lissen, man, I've been playing steadily in this club for three days and two nights, have to take speed to make it. Now, I can't sleep unless I get some valium. See?"

"That's a lousy way to treat your body. What about it's normal cycles?"

"Don't give me any of that guru shit. Maybe I should say a mantra. I just need some sleep and valium is the only way I can do it. I didn't ask for any fucking lectures. If you were any good, you'd be over where the money is, the last batch you gave me was ripped off by some prick on the job! I just need one to get to sleep. Oh FUCK YOU!"

* * *

The cop enters the bank and exchanges shots with a robber. He calls for help. People are locked in the vault. Robber is armed and dangerous, a chance to use all that jazzy law and order stuff we bought.

Bullhorn:

"Come out, we've got you surrounded. Come out peacefully. Heroic police crawl into the bank behind tank like steel push things backed by an army complete with steel helmets and a remarkable variety of lethal weaponry. The very latest models of everything. Enter the vault with no resistance, release the hostages, the bank robber had been killed in the first exchange with the policeman. "Those people had been held hostage for over two hours by a dead man." Classic example of overkill.

"Does it seem to you that things are getting steadily weirder?"

"I feel like I'm on the Titanic and someone has just yelled 'look out for the iceberg!'"

Queen Elizabeth II is at sea with fifteen hundred people, ninety-year-old Stokowski, Grace Kelly's uncle and various other notables.

"Give me $320,000 in small bills, or we'll set off a bomb on the ship."

"Have you notified people on board?"

"If we tell them, they might become alarmed. If we don't they might be angry. I think we'll tell them."

Far out, everyone in the world knows about the bomb except the people on the ship.

The President is preparing a trip to Moscow. Announcements of major areas of agreement to be dribbled out over the course of a week. Joint efforts to clean up pollution, medical team work to clean up cancer and heart disease; the old men still run the governments. Joint space ventures, U.S. and Russian space ships to link up in the void. Marriage of the giants consummated in the blackness of eternity, transmitted to the families in living color. Greatest sex show ever.

"We stand on the brink of peace in our time."

A large bomb goes off inside the pentagon. The natives are getting restless.

Wonder if he'll go by ship or by plane?

The wounded governor lies on the pavement oozing blood. Someone drops a handkerchief over the wound. Time passes, stand back, God help us, give him some air, please give us some room! Where's the ambulance? Maybe we shouldn't leave him on the ground like that? It's been a long time, where is the ambulance? The whole world is watching. Where is the ambulance? Put the poor bastard in a station wagon. Where in hell is the ambulance! Maybe he'll die before it gets here. There's the ambulance. What took you so damned long?"

PUTREFACTION . . . THE CORPSE IS BEGINNING TO SMELL.

"Man has achieved the power to create and to destroy matter. If he can regain his instinctual powers and retain self-consciousness, he will be a god."

THE FETUS IS BEGINNING TO STIR . . . QUICKENING.

Acupuncture demonstration at San Francisco General. It works just like they said!

"There are yin and yang meridians in the body. There are points along these meridians which are like energy sinks; these are the acupuncture points. They represent the areas where the energy of the TAO enters and leaves the body and connects with the various organs."

They take radial pulses and from the pulse character. They can determine the site and nature of the energy imbalance, pulsations of the blood in the arteries of the wrist are, after all, no more than manifestations in the living organism of pulsations of cosmic energy.

"The needles are inserted in such a way as to correct the blockage in the flow of energy. They are left in place for five to twenty minutes, and the area is massaged. In case the area of treatment is cold, we apply moxobustion."

CASE #1:

Tennis elbow in a doctor's wife. History of repeated cortisone injections, indocin tablets, physiotherapy, ultra sound, with no relief.

CASE #2:

Knee pain in a janitor. Same essential story.

CASE #3:

Back pain in a man with prostate cancer, spread to the spine.

All report significant relief of
removal.

"What makes the needles vibrate like th..

"The relief of pain will last for up to three days or
so, then the procedure is repeated up to twenty times.
The periods of relief of pain gradually increase after each
treatment, until it does not return."

CASE #4:

Mrs. Wong was diagnosed as having a herniated
disc. She underwent three operations without success.
Finally she developed an inflammation of the spinal
cord; arachnoiditis from the dye which was injected into
her back in the course of the examinations.

"The pain was excruciating and constant. I couldn't
sit up, my husband had to carry me to the bathroom, the
pain never left me. I thought about killing myself.
Finally I had this electrode implanted in my back with a
cord under my skin, over my shoulder to this sensor in
my chest so when I pushed the button on this box, I
would feel pins and needles in my back and the pain
would disappear for about one hour. After the first acupuncture treatment, the pain went away, and I haven't
had to use the box; after several treatments, I was able to
walk. I can now keep house, drive my car, and yesterday
I even played a game of ping pong."

* * *

*Two anesthesiologists in a classic sadomasochistic
relationship devise an experiment to administer a measured pain stimulus. A square wave of electricity which
causes painful muscle spasm and measure the voltage at
which he yells ouch. "This machine can cause enough
spasms to rip the muscle right off the bone." A quantita-
tive test of acupuncture anesthesia.*

"Hit me a few times to get a baseline voltage."

"My interest in this is the relief of pain. I invented this machine to produce pain in order to study it so I could relieve it more efficiently."

"Hit me just once more to make absolutely sure of that value."

The needles are left in place for twenty minutes. The machine reapplied. There is no increase at all in pain tolerance; he yells ouch at exactly the same voltage. The experiment is a failure. We leave to see a play in the park called the revenge of the Dragon Lady.

* * *

Meet Dr. John on the street; he's left the clinic and gone straight. Works in a VD clinic four days a week.

"Did some one call you about a wheezing baby in a solid gold room?"

His face darkens, becomes contorted and his body stiffens. Looks like smoke is about to come out of his ears.

"That one! She has this fancy pediatrician in the city, asks me what I think, then calls him. He always says the kid has something else and I don't know what I'm talking about. She just better not call me again, that one." He walks off muttering under his breath.

The room was painted over a week ago. Wonder what you dissolve gold in. She said she could still smell it.

"Take her out of the room and don't put her back until you can't smell the paint."

At the push of a button, electrically controlled doors open and a black Ferrari backs out into the street. Push the button again, the doors close. Wooden barn doors, yet.

"How's the baby?"

Push another button, the window of the black Ferrari slides down.

"It was an infection."

"Who said?"

"I called my pediatrician in the city and he said it couldn't be the paint. I took her in to see him the next day because she had a red ear."

"You think that breathing those fumes for a whole week had anything to do with it?"

"Well, he gave her an antibiotic. Do you think polyethelene covers on the wall will help?"

"She's back in the room?"

"My pediatrician in the city said there was no reason to take her out."

"Can you still smell that stuff?"

"It's still pretty heavy."

"Take her out of the room and don't put her back until you can't smell the paint."

"O.K. Thanks."

At that push of a button, the window of the black Ferrari glides up.

***

Felicity is from Berkeley. Used to be in advertising, wrote copy, now she runs the alpha machine . . . correlating wave production with subjective states. Says she had a schizophrenic episode.

"If you build it right, you can sit in a pyramid and experience the high the astronauts got from walking in space."

The astronaut who did the first space walk refused to come back onto the ship.

"If you don't come in now, we're gonna come out and get you!"

"It's the kind of high that makes people risk their lives to experience it."

* * *

A poet walks by, unsteadily, one eye open wide, the other closed down to a slit. He has an ulcer.

"I'm full of rum!"

"How does the world look to you?"

He raises his right fist into the air, and extends the middle finger and turns his hand so the palm faces toward himself.

"I have a set of instructions on how to build a pyramid."

Walking on the beach, Kevin finds a dead shark.

"I think I'll put it in a pyramid."

"What the hell for?"

"To preserve it. It seems that the shape has something to do with drying it out. If you have the right kind of pyramid, face it in the right direction, and put the thing inside in the right place, you get mummification. It will also sharpen razor blades; it's in the ancient writings. Look at the shape of a wizard's hat."

He leaves the shark on the beach.

He leaves town to join a healing commune up north.

* * *

Alan drops in on his way to a ball game.

"I just wanted you to meet my friend Tony. He's into pyramids. He'd like to rap with you about them, but we're late for the game; just wanted to get you two together."

"Hi, I'm Tony; I've been working with pyramids for several years now; I'd really like to talk to you about it, but we're late for the game. Soon . . . ."

"METAPHYSICAL MYSTERIES OF THE GREAT PYRAMID"

An article in a medical magazine. The pyramid of Cheops, faces precisely North-South. Side walls at an angle of 52 degrees, composed of stone blocks two to seventy tons each and so well fitted a knife blade won't fit between them. Forty stories high, width and height proportional to the distance between the earth and the sun. Inside dimensions indicate familiarity with the exact circumference and radius of the earth. Information we were not sure of until we were able to send ships into space. A scientist near the top of the great pyramid raises his hand, spreads the fingers, and hears a high pitched whistle. Drinking from his wine bottle, he gets an electric shock. Dead animals wandered in during the night, are thrown into trash barrels by the guards. In spite of the extreme heat and high humidity, there is no decay. They look like mummies. He builds a scale model and places it N-S and finds that dead matter placed inside does not decay. It seems to just dry out. He publishes his findings . . . "The pyramid seems to act as an accumulator of cosmic energies, the nature of which we are at present unaware." They may be as much as 10,000 years old . . . who built them? Are they the work of highly advanced cultures? Are occult and metaphysical writings the data collected and preserved by sophisticated scientists? These writings deal with cosmic energy, its nature and characteristics. Magic deals with practical applica-

tions of the creative cosmic energy. A milk company in Italy puts out a container in the shape of a pyramid and claims the contents do not have to be refrigerated. Shape power!

The author places a razor blade in a small pyramid.

"On examination after prolonged exposure, the blade edges showed striations and renewed sharp edges. I have gotten over 200 shaves out of one Gillette Blue Blade."

"The pyramid must be an accumulator of cosmic energies, the nature of which we are at present unaware."

In the 1940's Willie Reich made orgone boxes and people sat in them to accumulate "orgone energy." They put Willie away. He died in an institution . . . like Semmelweis who thought childbed fever was caused by microscopic organisms carried by surgeons who never washed their hands.

"Superstitious poppycock!"

A Czech patent is issued for a styrofoam "CHEOPS PYRAMID BLADE SHARPENER."

Someone makes a pyramid out of quartz. It transmits light. Observe behavior of light energy; get some clues. With the light source overhead, there appears in each corner a beam of light which is transmitted toward a space in the center, where the four beams join in a circle of light. "If the pyramid is tilted up on one edge the light passes through the bottom square, and at an angle of 52 degrees projects an image of a six pointed star onto the surface below."

"Is the doctor in?"

"He can't be disturbed . . . He's in the pyramid."

Politics

McGovern. . . bandwagon. . . screaming, swaying new people. . . superstar. . . religious fervor. . . a shoo-in for the Democrat nomination. . . The stock market drops precipitously. . . screaming, swaying old people. . . confrontation in Miami. . .

"We're opposed to violence! We just want to register our protest!"

"You are expecting maybe Abbie Hoffman leading hordes of Junkies high on LSD?"

"There's lots of sick older people in this town. Suppose someone is walking with a cane and he gets knocked over and has a heart attack?"

"Why can't they rent rooms, stay in hotels and be nice like normal people?"

"The reason many people are coming to the conventions is to protest the fact that they no longer can afford to rent rooms in hotels."

"If they can't afford it, they shouldn't come to Miami Beach. Lettem stay home!"

The rabble march out of the pages of history to pitch their tents on the golf course. $1000 fine for demonstrating without a permit. The police prepare. . . the councilmen argue. . . in Stockholm. . . U.N. commission on world ecology. . . Swedish president suggests that maybe destruction of Vietnam is ecologically unsound.

"Those remarks were biased, unsound, and are irrelevant to this forum."

The Russians do not send a delegate.

"We consider that there are matters at hand which are of greater import than the deteriorating environment of the planet."

The well-educated young son of a Japanese industri-alist and two of his friends attack unarmed fellow humans at an airport reception area with hand grenades and machine gun fire.

"It looked like a slaughter house! There was blood, bits of human flesh, parts of arms and legs strewn all over the floor."

An old Richard Conte movie comes next, about this place in ancient times called Babylon. The big scene in it is where a hand appears and writes a mysterious message on the wall of the king's dining room. Someone trans-lates the message:

"YOU HAVE BEEN WEIGHED IN THE BALANCE AND FOUND WANTING."

A CBS news analyst complains that "every event, no matter how trivial, is interpreted in cosmic terms." He sees no point to this; six weeks ago he saw no hope for the McGovern candidacy.

A scientist suggests the evolution of the noosphere of Chardin. A brain of the entire race of humanity in which each person represents one cell connected to the whole by means of the circumglobal TV computer network.

"This developing cortex of evolving humanity con-sists of two lobes. The one represented by inward looking Eastern philosophy, and the other by Western techno-logic materialism."

The six pointed star of the kabalah refers to the Hermetic axiom

"AS ABOVE, SO BELOW."

Concerning Reality

Walk down to the clinic along the beach, warm sun, the first real summer day.

"Hi, I hear you're going to Russia. Far out!"

She describes a discomfort in her abdomen which had been present for some time.

"I was sure it was something growing in there. I just kept after them until they agreed to operate and sure enough they found a tumor. I just absolutely knew it was there."

"You probably put it there. That's what the meeting in Russia is about."

***

"Did you hear about this guy in Italy who smashed up the Michelangelo 'Pieta' with a twelve pound hammer? He said he was the avenging angel of Jesus Christ out to wreak vengeance upon mankind."

***

"This is Charlene. You know Tina from the grocery? Well the guy she's been living with flipped his lid about a month ago. He's really crazy, threatening to kill people and stuff like that."

At the clinic are seated the relatives of the accused madman. Charlene comforts them. There is a hushed air of bereavement and worry over a critically ill loved one. Thomas, the brother; Tina, the old lady, arms wrapped around each other, weeping and consoling each other, rocking slowly back and forth.

"We just wanna do what's right. I can't even reach him any more. He says he'll kill me, he says he's Christ returned to earth after 2000 years. This time he's an avenging Christ whose mission it is to destroy those who do not truly follow the word."

"You just can't put somebody away for something he says."

"We'll just get a bunch of guys, and make him get into the car. He's pretty strong, but we can take him. He's my brother and I gotta do what's right."

"He'll thank you for it afterwards."

Gary walks in, a surfer, has a broken floating rib.

"You're talking about Matt, right? I've just come back from where he's at. I've been doing Kundalini yoga with a guru for some years now. Last week he turned on my abdominal, chest and throat chakras. He said he thought that was all I could handle at this time. I tell you, I was somewhere else for four days."

"Yeah, but Matt doesn't eat or sleep anymore."

"That's what happened to me, when you're on that plane of being you don't need any sleep. My old lady had to care for the body for four days and I was just travelling out on the astral plane all that time. When I came back it was to another level of existence."

"He just opened too much too soon. If you do that and leave your body before you know how to do it right, the body gets taken over by discarnate spirits looking for just such a chance."

"I think we can sort of talk to him and guide him back onto this plane."

Everyone agrees to bring him in on Thursday when the new walk-in group, sponsored by the county has its first meeting.

"We'll all have to go with him and talk it out good."

"Anyway you just can't lock him up because he says he's Jesus Christ. There's this weird trip about his civil rights."

"He probably really is Jesus, and he's getting about the same reception he did last time he visited us." Murray, about 55, a retired analyst, been working with psychotics for 25 years and quit last year to travel around the world. "Jesus was a practicing psychic; anyone can do what he did." He described a technique known as Silva Mind Control, developed in Texas by an unlettered Mexican laborer over a period of forty years.

"We show you how to get into the alpha state, how to stay conscious while you are. No trance, we teach you how to orient yourself in this state, and how to use it for astral travel, thought projection and reading, diagnosis and healing even at great distances, and how to return to this plane at will. The course usually takes a week. I think we can condense it to four days. We'll start tomorrow."

Walk back up along the beach after clinic. A large sand castle at the water's edge. Maximum expected life span is until the next high tide. Two, maybe three hours. Impermanence.

A bunch of baby crabs skitter toward the water's edge. New moon in Cancer, a new cycle, the sign Cancer refers among other things to the quantum jump by which energy evolves form one state of existence to another. People at clinic; four Cancer moons.

A nice looking young couple fucking on a deserted stretch of beach, sun in Gemini, the sign for the fusion of opposites which plants the seeds for evolution of the new cycle as it marks the death of the old cycle.

They never even noticed me walking by. None of them, did I make them all up?

"Consensus reality is a hologram projected in space."

It is projected by a biocomputer with three and a half million terminals. The biocomputer is programmed by conscious will. John Lilly calls it metaprogramming. Everybody always gets what he or she really wills. In order to reprogram, the computer must be put into a receptive state, the alpha state, no computer can be reprogrammed operating in the beta state. Attention fixed on the hologram 'out there.' *It is as real as you decide it is.* Ignore it, and you deprive it of its vital energy, it ceases to exist. Click. It's gone.

"Close your eyes, count backwards from three to one. Take a deep breath say each number as you exhale. See the number projected in your imagination, then turn your attention toward the harnessing of cosmic energy. Inward. "In here." Turn off the hologram, watch the images arise inside, light flashes, chains of little circles with dark centers. Colors go deeper, count backwards from ten to one. Take a deep breath and go deeper and deeper. The tape plays a tick tock at the alpha rate, eight to twelve cycles per second as the hologram disappears, the images become more distinct and brighter.

"See it, feel it, sense it, know it is real. It *is* real."

It is as real as you decide it is. DECIDE THAT IT IS REAL.

"If you want someone to be healthy, see them healthy. DECIDE THAT IT IS REAL. If you want money, see yourself spending it. IT IS REAL. The biocomputer will reproduce the program in the hologram 'out there,' if you believe that it will. It is programmed by the images we create 'inside.' "We are constantly programming our reality."

IT REALLY WORKS

"Try it, you'll like it."

Patrick joins the group.

"I just can't believe in that shit. It can't possibly be that easy."

Michael joins the group. He's a tantric master who used to work in a John Lindsay project in the NYC ghetto, spent a million and did nothing.

"You just can't reach samhadi in four easy lessons, it takes many many years of dedicated work and sacrifice."

Even if one has sought liberation for thirty-five life-times, when it occurs, it happens in an instant, like a lightning flash. A quantum jump.

At the end of the four day course, all twenty-five participants can do psychic diagnosis, and are able to control the hologram, affect the circumstances of their 'external reality.'

We will revise and retype the programming. The graduates of the four day wonder course will organize a course in "Psychic orientation through controlled imagery.."

***

"See the white king asleep in the sun. Let us awaken him so he won't get burned."

"He is dreaming and we are the people of his dream. If you wake him up, we shall all disappear."

Said the white queen to Alice . . . in Wonderland.

Einstein first turned us on to the idea that matter and energy are two aspects of the same phenomenon. $E = MC^2$. Matter becomes energy when you light a fire. Energy becomes matter in a cloud chamber. Thoughts radiate energy. Try sitting next to someone who's just had an argument.

"You guys on some kind of a psychic healing trip? My mother is critically ill, she's in New Jersey, nephrosis. She's all swollen up and they say her kidneys are shut down, and they think she won't make it. Is there something you can do for her?"

Twenty-five people put themselves into the state as directed, alpha.

"Visualize the body of A.S. in the V.A. hospital in New Jersey, see it, visualize it, know it is there. Know it is real. It is real...,,

Everybody sees a version of a round swollen body.

"Visualize her kidneys."

Imagery behind closed eyes organizes into two kidney like shapes. They are black, no energy or color in them, they are full and distended.

"See them, feel them, know they are real. They are real. Repair them. Visualize them as normal and functioning. All together, fix them in any manner, make them work."

Visualize a healthy red glow starting up in the kidney like shapes and make it real bright; the black color becomes liquid and runs down two ureter shaped tubes of light. The red shapes recede in size and take on a pink glow.

"Be nice if we had some feedback on this case."

Three days later, the son gets a letter from New Jersey. "I don't know what they did but at 5:00 p.m. our time on that day, my kidneys suddenly began to work and I passed 1000 cc of urine and my swelling is gone. I feel much better. Thank them for me. ...."

Our group did the session at 2:00 p.m. Pacific time. Synchroncity!

"The psychologists were not prepared psychologically or scientifically for what they saw. They rejected the evidence a priori."

***

In a program called "Countdown to 2001" it is noted that "the information and data brought back from the moon has already produced many facts which do not jibe with our accepted norms as to what constitutes reality."

***

In Moscow Dr. Naumov mentions an episode relevant to the development of parapsychology in the USSR. The Russian journalist, Vladimar Lvov, wrote a critical article in the English language "New Scientist." The result was a severe and adverse public reaction.

"Is this journalist one who is truly qualified to write about scientific experiments?"

In his coverage of scientific progress in the USSR for several foreign periodicals, Mr. Lvov made several statements.

"Show me only one convincing experiment on psychokinesis, and I will believe it exists."

"We have performed not only one, but many convincing psychokinetic experiments. These phenomena are repeatable. While some of the bioinformational (telepathic) phenomena are difficult to confirm, these psychokinetic experiments are definitely repeatable. The state of consciousness required is not as difficult to achieve. Our purpose is to search out the truth."

Ships and planes rain fire onto the east coast of Vietnam, hurricane Agnes like an avenging angel rains down water onto the east coast of the U.S., rivers rising at the rate of one and a half feet per hour, dams give way. Harrisburgh under 10 feet of water, Wilkes-Barre to be evacuated, one half million people washed out of their homes. The rain has stopped, the deluge, five states a disaster area. Worst disaster in history. It's still raining. Troops in Miami for the conventions, Dylan's hard rain?

"Malkuth hangs suspended from Yesod like a pendant." Malkuth, the world of the five senses. Yesod, the sphere of the psychic.

"The trouble is, that you still think there is a difference between the two."

Kelly has been a 'psychic' reader for about a year now. Her ability to see auras developed spontaneously.

"I thought I was going crazy! I saw this girl in the bank bending over a computer and suddenly there was this blaze of colored lights all around her."

She connects with a rag man in Berkeley named Lou. He teaches her how to control the flow of images and do 'readings.'

"If I want to know the number of children, I visualize a plant. The number of leaves is the number of children. It's always right."

If she has to do something and it worries her, she visualizes the situation.

"That way, when I get to do it, I'm not nervous because I've done it before and it is familiar."

She would like some 'legitimization.' She becomes director of psychic research for the clinic. She will do a research project on long distance diagnosis and healing. This seems to satisfy her Irish-Catholic morality which hangs around her neck like an albatross.

Felicity the egg magnate. She sells organic eggs to the local communes and health food stores, correlating brain wave states with drug states. Heroin puts you into delta, acid and pot into theta, speed into beta.

If you can induce the state, it won't be necessary to take the drug, maybe . . . .

Karl is working with a strobe light to find the frequency which will put people in a trance. Felicity is monitoring correlating brain wave frequency with subjective experience at different strobe settings.

"Alpha-shmalpha. I don't care a bit what they say. It's all hypnosis, Svengali was right."

Kelly suggests that we hypnotize people into a receptive state.

"Teach them how to do something in their own lives, so they can experience it directly. Select those that are capable and dedicated, form a healing circle, and amplify and direct the energy. Collect data on your results, publish the data, but just don't get caught up in it. Don't forget that you're just a channel for that power; whatever it is.

The ecology conference in Stockholm passes a resolution banning killing of whales for 10 years. There is banter in the streets about a resolution to ban the killing of humans for a period of ten years. THEY are an endangered species.

"It is very disturbing to me, emotionally, to think you can dismiss me as a figment of your imagination. If I took the final plunge into the depths you wouldn't pull me out."

"I'm just a hologram you made up to send a message from you to yourself. Maybe that's all that keeps you from taking the plunge."

Maya has visions which won't go away even when she opens her eyes. She is advised that her visions are at least as valid and real as ours.

"People are afraid to come to my house, they say strange things happen there . . . . Things are always falling down and hitting people at my house . . . ."

She smiles a bit . . . . . .

"People say that I'm doing it . . . with my mind . . . it really scares them . . . ."

She is describing spontaneous psychokinesis.

PSYCHOKINESIS *was discussed at the Moscow Conference on Bioenergetics and related phenomena, July 1972. The speaker was Dr. Edward Naumov of Moscow's Institute of Technical Parapsychology.*

"Psychokinesis is investigated in two ways."

The two main areas of research are with mediums and people with known psychokinetic ability, also with spontaneous occurrences. Spontaneous psychokinetic episodes have not been extensively investigated in the USSR, but Dr. Carger and Professor Bender of Germany have investigated these phenomena. Spontaneous PK is also known as poltergeist phenoma.

They have been working with a lady named Kulaguna. There is a film in which Kulaguna makes the needle of a compass spin in circles. She causes a pen to roll across a table in any direction simply by placing the open palm close to the object; it works with a cigarette as well. In some experiments, she did not use her hands. Her psychologic state during the experiment was that of stress.

Dr. Naumov took the film to a scientific meeting in Moscow:

"I didn't find any support in the ranks of the psychologists."

He did, however, find great interest among Russian physicists. A group of psychologists came to Moscow to investigate the Kulaguna phenomena.

Kulaguna came to Moscow for the experiments.

MOSCOW

REPORT OF PHYSICIST VICTOR ADAMENKO

In telekinetic experiments with Kulaguna, electrostatic fields were noted.

"It seemed as if unknown forces were at work."

Ability to move material objects with electrostatic force was of greater interest to physicists than to psychologists. A needle weighing one gram was balanced on a pivot and placed under glass and Kulaguna was able to generate enough electrostatic force to deflect the needle. It seemed easier for her to move objects when they were under a plastic shield and it seemed that she was able to create an electrically charged field around the objects. This phenomenon occurs spontaneously during electrical storms. Arrangements were made to telecast the phenomenon, but the cameraman freaks and refuses to film the experiment. An example of a physical phenomenon with psychologic results. It is possible to train the operator in PK!

"Just as we train sportsmen."

What are the possible mechanisms? It seems that by an act of will it is possible to change the electrical potential at the points of acupuncture. This results in a change in the electrical structure of the entire field.

"An electric charge can be transferred at will from the acupuncture points to the surface of the object."

This is responsible for the movement imparted to the test objects. Physiologic parameters of the operator were studied before and after the experiments: heart rate accelerated; EKG showed arrhythmia (cardiac). This limited the time of any PK performance to 30 seconds. Kirlian photos of acupuncture points of her palms in resting state showed multicolored sunburst patterns.

When she thinks about moving objects pattern changes to round regular circle of light around the fingertips. The height of the emission decreased; which points to a decrease in the energy field.

The blue green color noted at rest changes to splotchy red in areas when the operator imagines moving the objects. The energy quantum in the finger tip corona has been decreased and changed in character; this indicates a change in potential between the fingertips of the operator and the test object. The operator converts psychic tension into electrostatic energy; this charges the surface of the test object and causes it to move. Several different subjects were used with variable results. Some subjects were able to move ten gram objects. It is interesting to note that performance improves with practice. If two objects are placed in close proximity, she can move either one at will, and leave the other stationary. An electric potential of 10,000 volts/cm is recorded between hand and object.

Kirlian photograph—emanation of energy from human finger.

CONVERSATION IN TOURIST HOTEL LOBBY

Czech Physicist: "The aurograms show these light projections from the human body, about an inch or so above the skin."

British Mind Dynamics Magnate: "That's the aura?"

Czech Physicist: "We haven't proved that this is the aura, but it would be a reasonable assumption."

British Mind Dynamics Magnate: "The theosophists teach that man emanates four physical bodies . . . the physical flesh body; the mental body . . . of a finer nature, still physical; the emotional body; and the spiritual body, which is the finest of all . . . now when we photograph this thing, are we just photographing some other aspect of the physical form, which has nothing to do with the mind or the emotion or the spirit . . . just some energy emanating from the physical . . . . Are we kidding ourselves?" A lot of people are saying that this Kirlian photography is *not* photographing the mind or the emotion or the spirit.

Czech Physicist: "We are not able to disprove that it is a physical thing, but it is very difficult to explain all our data on the basis of this hypothesis." A healer was healing a wen, a lump of old cells on the skin. The healer states, and again we can't prove this, that he was sticking his nails into the acupuncture points in the skin, instead of needles. The next day, the wen was gone, so it looks like the healing was effective, probably through acupuncture. Here is a picture of the energy (he shows a Kirlian photo of the healer's fingertips, with the orange and blue corona). It was taken at the moment of healing."

101

He describes the apparatus.

"We have a box, built in Czechoslovakia, on top of it is this big copper plate. The circuitry generates 40,000 volts in this copper plate. This is in a photographic dark room, with the hands of the healer placed on a photographic plate. The plate is opened in the dark, and the finger of the healer is pressed onto the film. The 40,000 volts goes through the hand, down to the legs and into the ground, and the amperage is minuscule."

The conversation drifts to psychokinetic phenomena.

"We have recorded an energy potential of two million volts between the lips of a young married couple kissing. Again, no amps. We are dealing in extremely high voltages. If you want to get energy out of this system you have to transform down to lower voltages, and then you will get kinetic energy output on the other end, amps. If for instance, we transform 2,000 volts down to two volts, we receive an energy flow of four amps. You can feel this. The healer feels it in his finger tips; there is actual radiation of energy, for this is a physical phenomenon."

"It is like making a car go. In this major function are many little functions, like turning the ignition key, creating a spark, transferring the power to the wheels, etc. Many minor functions go into making up the main function of imparting kinetic energy to the car. Our bodies are the same; we have many fine functions, and these go into lower and lower frequencies. And all of a sudden the body walks. This is all one; as soon as you start separating, you are lost. You must accept wholeness, not separation. The unity. Everything works as a wholeness, and not as separated parts."

British Mind Dynamics Magnate: "As I see it, you can say either everything is physical or everything is spiritual, it doesn't matter. It's all the one substance, just vibrating at different rates. There's only one substance, you see, in different manifestations. Words are so limiting here."

A German Engineer: "You can buy these machines on the open market in America. The Kirlian photo device, it is more a pseudo Kirlian device, is a beauty electrolysis machine. It is used to take out the hair on the face of a woman and it makes 25,000 volts in the treatment rod. You connect a wire to a copper plate from this rod in a dark room and lay polaroid color film on the plate, press the finger onto the film and run the current for 60 seconds."

Czech Physicist: "You can run the wire from the rod to the metal polaroid colorpack, take the pack off the camera, expose it to the current, put it back into the camera, pull over the rollers, and there you have the picture."

This bioplasmic energy which is being photographed is the ground substance of the cosmos. It is pure vibration which by lowering its frequency becomes the entire electromagnetic spectrum, and by lowering it still further becomes matter.

Czech Physicist: "Physically speaking, you cannot receive any frequency unless you are attuned to it. You can't get an FM station on an AM radio receiver. The whole question resolves down to what you got, that you can receive. If you can alter the frequency of your receiving organism you can get interesting results. The higher the frequency you tune to, the finer are your results. The frequencies manifest by the vibrating bioplasmic energy are endless. There are those who say that we have seven subtle bodies, with fine, finer and finest vibratory rates; I believe this to be incorrect. It is like looking through an electron microscope. The further you magnify, the more there is to see, it is infinite. When we speak of frequency, we imply different dimensions of reality; that jar represents a frequency rate which we call the world of atoms and matter. In any case, we no longer recognize the concept of 'physical things.' Materialization can take place under certain conditions but even in the material state, everything is a manifestation of this energy, this force. The concept of separately existing material 'things' is an illusion."

The smallest particle of ultimate reality seems to be vibrating between energy and matter. It is called a 'wavicle'; part wave and part particle. In terms of matter, it vibrates between existence and non-existence. Now you see it; now you don't. Force and form are the two ultimates. All existence vibrates between these two poles.

"The Russians showed Dr. Tiller a leaf which had been cut in half. Kirlian photos of the leaf that shows the half which had been cut away maintained its original shape in the Kirlian photos, even though it was no longer physically present. Dr. Tiller believes that this only occurs at certain frequencies, and the harmonic."

American Professor of Engineering: "It stands to reason. You are basically lighting up an energy, like lighting a light bulb. If you hit it with the right amount of energy, it lights up. You are talking about an energy envelope which exists whether the physical piece is there or not. At the right level, you light up the bulb and you see the filament. This is an analogy which makes sense."

American Doctor: "Another analogy would be phantom pain, where you get strong impulses from an amputated limb."

Engineering Professor: "Exactly. Because the energy envelope is still there. Isn't this an energy transmission? A pain is a communication, apparently from that envelope. When you speak of communication that puts us back on a common basis which we can then use . . . ."

Czech Physicist: "In our country we are interested in potential uses for this energy. It is definitely different and infinitely more powerful than electricity. If we had the proper tools, we could measure the amount of energy required for a plant to grow one inch; you could measure the energy frequency of an insect. We believe this is the energy which was harnessed by the pyramids. It is a newly discovered energy source, the energy of the universe. It is radiated to us by the sun and stars. Our bodies absorb it like a sponge and we then transform it into a suitable frequency so that it works. This may sound strange, but I even heard a Yogi say this. The Chakras are involved in this."

American Doctor: "Out of Sight."

Czech Physicist: "The energy was always there, 2,000, 100,000 years ago. Like electricity, it was always there. The problem is to concentrate it, direct it. We don't produce electricity, we concentrate something which was always there. Look, we can get power from a vacuum because air likes to rush into it. An electric generator is nothing but a vacuum machine. The electricity which is bound likes to become free again and it can do this by passing through a motor, an electric motor. This is an energy system. If we could do this with the energy which comes from the stars, use it like we use electricity, we could measure the frequencies of stones, plants or anything you like. You could measure the pulse of a fly. It would then become clear what our bodies are, structurally and functionally. The Czech people realize that electricity is a limited source of power. You cannot use it for everything. You cannot use it for growth but think of the power of growth."

American Doctor: "Growth is an energy transformation. We transform the energy of the sun into protoplasm, into the matter of our physical bodies so to speak."

Czech Physicist: "There are billions of stars out there, and they all radiate energy. Let us assume that our physical body as we see it has seven finer bodies. The finest body has the same frequency as do the stars. That is what connects us to the cosmos. We absorb the energy when we attract it by vibrating at the same frequency. Then we transform it."

British Mind Dynamics Magnate: "Did you say we had seven bodies?"

Czech Physicist: "In our sun system, everything is in terms of seven. There are other sun systems; the factor is twelve in many of them. In music if the tone is not in harmony with the one in a higher octave, you get dissonance which has destructive effects."

British Mind Dynamics Magnate: "I don't understand that."

Czech Physicist: "Disharmony creates waves of a destructive nature."

American Doctor: "Disharmony destroys the form and releases the energy. Cosmic force becomes molded into form which it must destroy in order to create new forms."

Czech Physicist: "Like fire in which the trapped energy becomes free again."

Someone mentions work in Italy where they are photographing thoughts and taking pictures of the past; the work is highly secret because they are on the verge of fulfillment and do not want to arouse premature publicity. An English lady states that she can believe anything but that. She is advised that it is not a matter of belief, but one of investigation to determine the truth. It is suggested that if consciousness is sufficiently expanded, the past and the future are seen to be functions of the present, extensions of the present instant, which contains all time. If we can get above our three dimensional finite body and mind like in an airplane, we can see past, present and future at one time.

"The ancient prophets went back into their minds at night so they could see into the future. They understood there is only one time and that is the now."

English Lady: "I don't doubt that they could see into the future, I just don't think one can photograph the future."

British Mind Dynamics Magnate: "What's the difference? If you can see into the future, why can't you photograph it?"

English Lady: "I can't imagine how they would actually do it."

Czech Physicist: "On what does the future depend? This involves the concept of Karma. A thought is a living substance . . . maybe thousands are produced each minute. Each has its own existence, and creates its own reality . . . in time . . . . The future is born at the same instant as the thought."

American Doctor: "Thoughts program the biocomputer. The biocomputer projects the hologram we call reality. Whatever series or arrangements we make with our thoughts actually create the hologram, reality. It manifests faithfully, like protoplasm manifesting the DNA code in genetics. The biocomputer is the brain, and the printout is on the consciousness."

Czech Physicist: "From beginning to end, we are creators, that is our God like aspect. We need this understanding in order to achieve perfection in our creations. This is where we are learning; this is why we are here."

American Engineering Professor: "Do we create, or do we reflect a creative energy?"

Czech Physicist: "If we create in ignorance, then we suffer through illness, accidents, and so forth. Thought forms always crystallize into our experience. This is a cosmic law."

British Mind Dynamics Magnate: "I certainly agree with that. We are a creative force. We do it with the power of our minds to make images. Those images become reality so we can create anything we want, actually; through the force of our own imagination."

BACK IN BOLINAS

JIM: "The psychobiophysiocosmologaphere. Good health means creating it, i.e., the illusion, and not only letting the illusion create you, or in more practical terms, this can be interpreted to mean that the phenomena of health on some plane is manifested by taking responsibility for your own self, existence in the psi-sphere."

Jim started a free clinic in Chinatown. He turned it over to the local people. Long hair, a Lincoln like beard, baggy orange printed pants.

"I like my balls to hang free."

He has a copy of an interoffice memo from St. Mary's Hospital in S.F. re: Orange Pants While on Duty.

"I can't help it! I'm fucked up! I can't help it if I'm fucked up, can I?"

He joins the clinic. A group of people in a commune take him in.

"I'm sharing a room with an 8-year-old. It's really far out."

He buys the house, the commune people have to move out.

"I know, I'm obnoxious. Fucked up, too."

"You don't do it, it does you. There's nothing to do."

He demands to know from every patient why they created their symptoms. He does this in his orange pants and baggy white shirt. He inspires little confidence.

"Are you sure that character is really a doctor?"

* * *

"SYMPTOMS OF ILLNESS ARE LIKE THE RED OIL LIGHT IN YOUR CAR. THEY LET YOU KNOW SOMETHING IS WRONG WITH YOUR THINKING, WITH YOUR PICTURE OF REALITY. WESTERN

MEDICINE RESPONDS TO THIS BY RIPPING OUT THE OIL LIGHT. THEY REMOVE THE WARNING SIGNAL AND ALLOW THE DESTRUCTIVE PROCESS TO CONTINUE UNCHECKED."

* * *

"Look, man, I have this gingivitis, swollen gums. See? I have to leave for London in two hours. I always get gingivitis when I'm under stress, and the doctor always gives me penicillin when I get nervous so I won't get gingivitis."

"I don't think penicillin is indicated for simple nervousness."

"Another one of your lousy space raps, up yours, mother."

She storms out.

Then one day, Jim cuts his hair, puts on a striped button down shirt, a muted purple jacket and a white coat with his name emblazoned in plastic over his breast.

"I'm through being fucked up."

The pictures of Buddha, the ethereal poems, the astrology charts come down. Diplomas, practice licenses, and sundry other impressive documents set in permanent plastic go up.

The picture of Christ, the antique dissection mannekin and the Celtic cross remain on the piano.

* * *

Jim calls his father in New Jersey.

"I'm not coming back to set up practice in Newark."

"I bought this house here, I can see the sun come up through one window and it sets in the other window. I walk to work along the beach every day, along the seashore. It's beautiful, I love it."

"What did he say?"

"He said I'm killing my mother,..?"

Jim sweeps the pile of freshly cut hair into an envelope, seals it, and mails it home without any covering letter.

"Lilith. That's who she is. LILITH is running wild. Have you noticed that?"

"Think of it as theatre," says Pearlie.

She refuses the lead in "Mother Courage" because she is already in a play. 'Mother Courage' with a dash of 'Antigone.'

"Shit on the audience!" says Peter. He draws little sketches in a hard covered book with lines. In German he captures his thoughts. He builds puppets, up to fifteen feet tall. In puppets he captures his imagery. God Creating the World. Peter creating a play.

"AS ABOVE SO BELOW," says Hermes, an Egyptian who lived a long time ago.

In what is presented as "A clear choice between good and evil," Tricky Dicky was reelected by a landslide. AMERICA declares herself overwhelmingly on the side of evil.

"I would definitely advise that you prepare to leave this plane as soon as possible."

In her meditations, Kelly has created a reality which is as compelling and convincing as that of the five senses.

"You just use any of the standard Buddhist or Tibetan techniques. One pointed concentration is good, first the 'out there' gives way to the 'in here.' I sort of rush back from time to time to make sure it is still 'there.' That's stage one. After that awareness of the body disappears, that's a realy scary part, right there, you feel that you are being taken over. You're beyond emotion at this point; no feelings at all, just an awareness of a force turning you back, back into the body. If you are really determined to get out of this plane, you get back to that point. You find that after about five or ten minutes you get past it. Then you are on another plane. It's beautiful . . . fantastic . . . glorious . . . ."

We walk along the edge of the ocean. The sun turns the sky pink. She shows no sign of emotion.

"I'm really tired of the senses, I'd like to leave. I've been on the other plane only two times now, about an hour each time. The form is completely different. I'm just getting to find my way around.

She is creating form on a new plane.

"All I know is that when I'm there, I really see no reason to come back. When I'm here, I can find no reason to stay. The psychic thing is kind of a stepping stone out of this level. I don't want to get hung up there either; I am determined to go higher."

The power of her will is the force which she is converting into new form. She agrees that the pictures in her head which foretell reality probably create that reality.

"It's probably true, but what does it matter. This

body is a fantastic machine to trip around in, on this plane. We're supposed to do that to get experience and move on to another level. We're just little creators. There is a higher power. We can't ever know what that is. That's what we have to stay in touch with, those mind control people. They don't understand . . . ."

"Let me know before you go, I'd like to talk with you at least one more time."

"I can't, I have to leave right now."

"I just love doing readings for people, they're like different parts of my own self, come to give me a message."

She has decided that she will return to this plane for a while longer.

"The plane of the senses is like a school for us. We have to master it before we can move higher. Would you like to stay for Thanksgiving dinner? We're eating at five."

Four Jesus Freaks blow into town one day. They knock about for a while, praising the Lord Jesus. They move into the minister's house . . . "in the name of Jesus" and they offer guitar lessons. They offer Friday night bible readings for youth, they administer the free box, they watch a couple of psychic tuning sessions, they litter the minister's house, and they tell the five little old ladies, "Those people are going about the work of the devil!" They ride out of town to continue the work of Jesus.

* * *

Dr. Jim starts wearing ties and $200.00 silk suits around town. A lady minister comes from the big city to reassure the five little old ladies.

"No, they are not preaching Christian teachings in the clinic. That is the work of a minister, and I for one would resent their doing it."

"No, they are not spreading anti-Christ doctrines. I myself have taken the Mind Control course."

Dr. Jim incurs the wrath of the local women.

"He treated my kid's tonsilitis ok, but he kept rubbing his balls up against me all the time he was doing it."

"I saw him in a book shop in Berkeley. This girl said hello to him and he grabbed her right in the crotch! In a crowded store! Blew her right out, she didn't know what to do."

He claims he was just doing God's work as he rides out of town on the back of a motorcycle.

"Do you know where Shalom went? That bastard made $30 worth of calls on my phone and then left town!"

He was fucking her, too. Did you know Dr. Jim had an alias?

"I asked him if he remembered the part in the Oath of Hippocrates where it says that you're not supposed to fuck your patients."

"He said he never did it in the office."

* * *

KELLY CALLS

"I'm in this healing group. We meet once a week at this psychiatrist's house."

"Do you use imagery?"

"No, I work on the aura. I manipulate the colors in my head. It seems to work well, but the only problem is that two weeks ago I got a sore throat, and last week I got laryngitis."

"Rolling Thunder says that's one of the dangers of healing. You need a ritual to throw off the illness after it leaves the patient. He burns a piece of meat in the fire and then vomits. Sucking healers generally use this technique."

She will experiment with different rituals and report her results.

* * *

"Can you guys help me? I lost my memory, can't even remember what day it is, or anybody's name. Can you guys help me get my memory back?"

His name is Tim, about 25, barefoot, disheveled, with warm, trusting eyes. He got a medical discharge after sustaining a head injury in Vietnam.

"I went to the V.A. Hospital in this other state, I don't remember which one. I asked them to help me get my memory back. They locked me up, wouldn't even let me out of the building. I escaped, came out here, is this the free clinic?"

"That's far out. No past, no future, you just live in the instant. Discontinuous, egoless, nirvana."

"How do you like it?"

The glow in his eyes becomes more intense as he shakes his head up and down happily.

"I love it. It's fantastic."

"People starve themselves and sit in caves for twenty years at a time trying to get where you're at, and here you are trying to get yourself cured of it. People sure are weird. Why do you want to change it if it's so great?"

"I have trouble getting around. I keep forgetting where I am and why."

Jesse starts him soaking his infected feet in a solution of phisohex, as Patrick discusses his own head injury and subsequent loss of memory.

"It was a state I had never experienced before; it was like a part that I had before was missing. I lost a whole section of my being. I wanted it back just because it was mine, or me, all that life up to the instant of the smashed skull. Crunch. It's gone . . . Better to forget it, let it go. To look back is to be imprisoned by who you were before. Start each day with total amnesia, no ego. Out of sight!"

Tim is advised to identify himself as archtypical human, the product of four and a half billion years of cosmic evolution.

He moves into a two story treehouse by the beach and sets up housekeeping. He gets a flute and learns to play it. He smiles a great deal.

"I don't believe he's lost his memory at all," says Patrick.

Big G, the Kundalini student who had his chakras opened by his teacher and was out of his body for four days, walks in the front door, falls on the floor, and proceeds to writhe in agony. He is on his right side with his knees pulled up in fetal position. The pain awakened him this morning. He hasn't been able to piss since last night. Radiation of pain to the right testicle, percussion tenderness over the right kidney, point tenderness over the right ureter, kidney stone. The closest thing to childbirth a male human can experience. A small jagged stone in a tiny muscular urine conduit. It must travel down to the bladder and from there to birth at the end of the urethra. As it moves, it tears at the delicate tube wall, agonizing pain, bloody urine, when it stops moving it stops hurting. The pain indicates progress. There is no Demerol. He pleads for relief.

"Can you get out of your body at will?"

He nods his head and lies on the bed, face up.

"Instruct your body to pass the stone. Stay on the other plane until it drops into the bladder. You can come back then."

He stares at the ceiling and within thirty seconds he is quiet and completely relaxed. Half an hour later he stands up.

"I'm ok now, the pain is gone."

An hour after that, the ambulance arrives. They went twenty miles in the wrong direction, at $5.00 per mile. The stone passes spontaneously and he has it in a bottle.

The prisoners come home from Vietnam. 1965 men in spiffy new uniforms strut proudly into 1973 America, saluting their God, their Country, and their President.

"Thank you, Mr. President, for bringing us home," says a proud American warrior.

"You can't go home again," says a famous American author.

Rip Van Winkle returns to industrial Japan after wandering in the jungle for twenty-five years. Another interface develops as modern man meets tribal man in Brazil, after thousands of years of isolation.

Sit in front of the TV and watch time melt away . . . in super chromacolor.

Physicists are postualting that time can, under some conditions, flow backwards. The President cuts all social welfare programs, moves toward one man rule, and announces 'an end to permissiveness.' The Haight Ashbury Clinic closes for lack of funds. Day Care centers close. Blue Cross holds up our Medi-Cal payments for six months. The Headlands Healing service closes for lack of funds. POOF! . . . It's gone.

Thus the Superior man
Understands the Transient
in the Light
of
the Eternity of

THE END

I Ching

AFTERWORD

Jack Benny is gone, the Beatles are gone, as is the Twentieth Century. Louis Armstrong summed it up when he described the intensive care unit in which he hovered on the brink of death amongst the bewildering array of tubes, switches and exotic electronic gadgetry, "Everybody is very nice in this place, only there isn't any music." A reasonable criticism from a dying man, and an illuminating insight into the attitude of some of my colleagues toward their fellowman; an attitude which seems to be rapidly changing as the fund-raisers turn their attention in 1976 from "community-run" health centers to "holistic" health centers. *Holistic health—* that's a turn-of-the-century euphemism for what we physicians used to call *general practice* and what patients used to call *caring.*

During Yule of 1974, the *five little old ladies* dealt with the Headlands Clinic as they had dealt with the morality plays from La Mama Theatre. Hiring the prestigious firm of P AND P ATTORNEYS to expel the Headlands Clinic from the church manse, they charged that we had allowed weeds to grow up behind the butane tank. It was also charged that various disreputable-looking characters were seen frequenting the premises. I must admit to both offenses. We mistook the weeds for blue flowers and the disreputable-looking characters were patients. The minister, assuming the role of probation officer testified that he had indeed seen disreputable characters entering the clinic.

About this time Jesse heard rumors that the *five little old ladies* believed we were doing the work of the devil in there. One day she saw a huge man with a huge cross around his neck in the process of exorcising our evil spirits. In the face of these events and a court order to vacate the premises, we decided to close the Headlands Clinic.

Out there in Walter Cronkite-land the apocalypse rages with increasing fury. Fifty-thousand-dollar-a-year executives are facing welfare, Catholics are killing Protestants, Christians are killing Moslems as Herr Kissinger mucks around in Angola and the Washington marches start again. Jack Rosenberg changes his name to Werner Erhardt and mesmerizes millions as did the Führer for an opposite (or was it the same) purpose. Fred Leboyer surfaces in Paris to claim that birth does not have to be pain and suffering. A patient tells me in Santa Cruz, "We are in the birth canal, and have taken some beating around but no damage has been done. I think we'll make it. . ." We only have to know that.

*The Universe knows what it's doing
and it means us no harm.*

BIRTH AND REBIRTH

birth
death
two sides
of the same entity—birthdeath

one cannot be born
until one dies

to die
is to be born anew

to be born
is to die to all that went before

a birth
2000 years ago
200 years ago
every second
we are born
we increase and die

what if . . .
we entered in joy
and left in contentment
deliciously satisfied
with ourselves and our life

can you imagine?

I cannot
but dare to hope
putting tentative footsteps on the path
wondering/ hoping/ wanting to believe

Darla Chadima—1975
Continuing Education Specialist
Human Development
University of California
Santa Cruz

OTHER BOOKS FROM CELESTIAL ARTS